HAND-CRAFTED BOATS OF OLD CURRITUCK

FISHING & BOATING ON THE CAROLINA COAST

TRAVIS MORRIS

Charleston · London
THE History PRESS

Published by The History Press
Charleston, SC 29403
www.historypress.net

Copyright © 2014 by Travis Morris
All rights reserved

First published 2014

Manufactured in the United States

ISBN 978.1.62619.648.3

Library of Congress CIP data applied for.

Notice: The information in this book is true and complete to the best of our knowledge. It is offered without guarantee on the part of the author or The History Press. The author and The History Press disclaim all liability in connection with the use of this book.

All rights reserved. No part of this book may be reproduced or transmitted in any form whatsoever without prior written permission from the publisher except in the case of brief quotations embodied in critical articles and reviews.

I dedicate this book to my second wife, Jo Ann Hayman Morris. Her first husband, Jimmy Hayman, died in 1986 when he was forty-four years old. My first wife, Frances Meiggs Morris, died in 1992 when she was fifty-seven years old. Jo Ann and I were married in 1995. I am ten years older than Jo Ann.

When Jo Ann was a little girl, I was dating her older sister. Jo Ann would be out in the field digging for crawfish, or fishing at Mill Landing if she could get anybody to take her there. In later years, I farmed the field across the road from where she lived on Maple Road. I had watermelons planted over there, and I told her she could have all of them she wanted. The watermelons were too heavy for her to carry, so she would roll them across the road. She still loves watermelon and eats it every day in the summertime if she can get it.

When I used to keep my hunting rig at Casey Jones' dock in Waterlily, Jimmy Hayman kept his rig there. I would see Jo Ann there before daylight on cold blustery mornings with Jimmy and sometimes Newton Hampton and Graham Keaton if they were going in the float box. I used to think it would be nice to have a wife that would go duck hunting with you. One never knows what life holds in store.

Before we got married, Jo Ann would go hunting with me, but soon after we were married, she'd say there were no ducks or the weather was too pretty or some other excuse. Age could have something to do with it.

Once we went on a cruise, and men were shooting skeet off the fantail of the ship. They were not hitting them too good, so I talked Jo Ann into shooting. The men that had been shooting kinda' smiled when she said she wanted to shoot. When she started shooting, it wiped the smiles off their faces…she was busting every one of those skeet!

When I was driving the truck for my son and was leaving home around midnight, sometimes I'd forget something and have to go back home. I always called before I went in the house because I knew Jo Ann had her shotgun right beside the bed and wouldn't hesitate to use it.

She does still like to go rock fishing with me, but she only wants to go when the season is in so she can keep them. She doesn't like to throw them back. She likes to eat them, and she's afraid she may be tempted not to throw them back and get in trouble.

Jo Ann has been very supportive of my book writing and promotes them in her hardware store, Hayman's.

Jo Ann Hayman Morris, reading a newspaper in the cabin of *Mother Goose*. I had my float box tied on the Gull Rock, and I was waiting on two members of Piney Island Club in the float box. This was the last time I ever tied my float box on the Gull Rock. I and several other members of the club had bought 125 Herters canvasback decoys we had tied out around that rig, plus about 75 geese. Two game wardens came out there just to look at that rig (so they said). I think one was Freddie Hampton. *Author's collection.*

Contents

Acknowledgements	7
PART I: BOATING AND FISHING IN OLD CURRITUCK	9
Long Net Rigs at Currituck Wharf	14
Bootie Spruill: Haul Net Fishing in Currituck Sound	20
Others Bootie Fished With	22
Carp	24
Mullet Fishing	24
My First Gas Boat	25
Vernon Lee Creekmore	26
Bell's Island Club	28
Laydown and Sit-Up Boxes	29
Mill Landing, Maple: Charlie Snowden	30
Edgar O'Neal Sr.	33
Maple Warehouse Company	33
Buck Allen	34
Henry Doxey	34
Gilman Brumsey	35
C.G. Wallace	36
Ambrose Dozier	36
Coinjock: Pat O'Neal	37
Elijah Tate	44

Contents

Riley Beasley	51
Next Bad Night in the Sound	55
Bob Morse	57
Albert Sumrell	61
Point Harbor: Allen Hayman	62
Wilton Walker	62
Newton Hampton	65
Carl Ross	70
Shoving Poles	72
Other Boats	73
PART II: COMMERCIAL FISHING ON THE OUTER BANKS	80
Buddy Ponton's Story	82
PART III: HUNTING AND FISHING LODGE ON MAINLAND CURRITUCK	102
Caroland Farm	102
Sportsman's View, by Purcell Kimsey	110
Bootie Spruill on Guiding Fishing Parties	125
About the Author	128

Acknowledgements

I wish to thank the following people for their contributions of time, stories and pictures:

- Buddy and Annie Ponton for the time they spent with me talking about commercial fishing on the beach, as well as the pictures they shared.
- Dorothy Grandy for the stories and pictures of Caroland Farm Hunting and Fishing Lodge.
- Bootie Spruill for the stories he shared with me about commercial and sport fishing and Susie Spruill for the pictures she shared of commercial fishing.
- Henry Doxey for the stories he shared about running the old Tom Brumsey boat for Charlie Snowden and other stories about Maple.
- Newton Hampton for his stories and pictures on boat building.
- Carl Ross for his stories and pictures on boat building.
- Glenna Walker Alcock for the pictures of boats that her daddy, Mr. Wilton Walker, built. She shared them with Wilson Snowden, who, in turn, shared them with me.
- Larry Woodhouse for the names of some people around Grandy who built boats.
- Susan Joy Davis. She is the person who got me started writing books; she is my sounding board. I know I can ask her something, and she will tell me what she thinks, not just what I want to hear.

Acknowledgements

- My daughter Ruth Morris Ambrose. When I can't spell a word good enough to get in spell check (which is quite often), I call Ruth. When I was in college, I wrote my daddy a letter, and he sent me back a book with 20,000 spelling words, but I don't think it helped much.
- Last but not least, my daughter Rhonda L. Morris. She doesn't look at the manuscript until I send it to the publisher to see if they are going to publish the book. Then I turn it over to Rhonda for editing and getting it in the form the publisher wants it in. She knows how I talk and can get it in their format without changing the meaning of what I'm saying. If an editor from the publisher did this work, I probably wouldn't recognize it. Rhonda has a full-time job as director of Kids First Child Abuse Treatment Center in Elizabeth City. She lives next door to my office, and I know she doesn't have much spare time, but she has always managed to find time to edit my books. I can write books, but I can't get them in the form the publisher wants them in. If it were not for Rhonda, these books wouldn't happen.

If I have overlooked anybody, it was not intentional, and I thank you also.

PART I
BOATING AND FISHING IN OLD CURRITUCK

I've loved boats all my life. When I was a little boy and we lived in the village of Currituck, Mama would send me to Mr. Henry Snowden's Store to get ten cents worth of meal, and I'd slip down to the wharf before I came home. I got more spankings over that than anything else I can remember.

The county wharf was where the ferry dock is now. This was a long wharf that had a slight curve to the south near the end.

On the north side of the wharf, there were several fish houses. As I recall, these belonged to Charlie Snowden, Mr. Earl Snowden and Mr. Lou Brumsey. Mr. Wallace Davis may have had one at one time (I know he had a fishing rig), and there were probably others. In between the fish houses were racks for drying the cotton nets. There was no such thing as nylon or monofilament nets back then. There was one little house that was built just for ice. It was just a little house with double walls and sawdust in between the walls for insulation.

There were three carp pounds (impoundments: enclosed areas in the water to keep the fish or turtles alive, yet unable to escape) and one turtle pen I remember. When the fishermen came in, they would have the carp in a carp car. They would pull it up on a ramp so the water would run out, put the carp in fish boxes, weigh them and dump them in the carp pound.

A carp car was basically a little skiff decked over with two lids that would open so the carp could be taken out. The sides and top of the little skiff, or "car," were bored full of holes so it would fill with water. When they caught the carp in the fish net, they would put them in the carp car to keep them alive, and they would tow this carp car along with the skiff that held the net. There was a little ramp beside the wharf that they pulled the carp car up on. This way the water would drain out and make it easier to get the carp out.

Every so often, a truck with a tank of water would come to pick up the carp and take them live to Fulton Fish Market in New York City. I've been told a rabbi would bless them before the Jews ate them.

The way they caught the fish in the carp pound was they had a net the width of the impoundment, with small enough mesh not to gill the carp. Two fishermen, one on each end of the net, would get overboard (the water was not too deep) and pull this net up toward the wharf end of the pound to crowd the fish up so they could be dipped up with a big dip net. Then they'd be put in fish boxes, weighed and put in the tank truck.

There was another wharf and carp pen just south of the county wharf. This was right behind Mr. Ed Johnson's store. It was called Johnson's Wharf. There was a deep hole between the county wharf and Johnson's carp pen. This was caused by the gas boats. All except Mr. Earl Snowden's boat were hooked up straight. By "hooked up straight," I mean she had no transmission; when you hit the starter, she went (at least you hoped she did). Mr. Earl's was the only one that had a marine transmission. This caused a high shoal to be next to Johnson's carp pen. Boys and girls swam down there a lot in the summertime. Some of the boys would dive off the fish house in the deep water, and some would play around on the shoal.

The fishing rigs were what we called long net rigs. The nets in later years would be about nine hundred yards long. If I remember correctly, that was as long as the law would allow later on.

The way this worked was like this: the captain picked the hauls (where he was going to run the net) and ran the gas boat. There would be two men in the skiff, one on either side. One was there to pull the lead line, and one was to pull the cork line. Of course, the skiff was tied to the gas boat.

When the captain got to where he was going to make the haul, the other two men would get in the skiff and stick the staff down (a long stick or "spud," with one end of the net tied to it). Now the captain would start the boat. Remember that most of the gas boats were hooked up straight, so the boat took off as soon as it was started. The nets had sticks about every eight feet to hold the cork line and lead line apart. The two crew members that handled these lines stayed in the back of the skiff to keep the sticks from getting hung up going out over the stern. It was very important not to get hung up in the net while it was going out or you'd go overboard, too (as you will find out later in a story by Bootie Spruill). After the net was run out,

Currituck Wharf. Cecil Sears' house boat is at the end of the wharf. His pulling boat is in the foreground, and the fishing skiff is anchored out. Note the nets piled up on the net rack to dry. *Wayne Taylor.*

Currituck Wharf. On the right is what is left of Johnson's wharf and carp pen. This is where the dock for the ferry to Knott's Island is today. *Author's collection.*

Bootie Spruill's fishing rig, ringing around taking in the haul seine. *Susie Spruill.*

Bootie Spruill. *Susie Spruill.*

Above: Carter Lindsey, with Lou Brumsey's gas boat in the background at Currituck Wharf. Note the curve in Currituck Wharf. The poles are for drying nets. *Wayne Taylor.*

Left: This picture shows how net was carried in the stern of the big skiff with the fish in the bow. *Susie Spruill.*

the two men would get back in the gas boat and usually sit in the lee of the cabin, where it was warmer, while the net was being pulled back around to the staff. If the net got hung, they would untie the skiff, stick a spud (long pole with a pointed end) down and tie the skiff to it, then take the gas boat and go back and unhang the net. After they got the net unhung, they would come back and tie the skiff back to the gas boat and keep pulling on the net until they got back to the staff.

When pulling in the net, the skiff would be turned sideways. A line that ran under the skiff would be tied to the bottom of the staff, and another line would be tied to the staff at the top of the net and fastened to the washboard. Another line ran from the middle of the skiff to the gas boat. Now they would do what they called "ring around." The gas boat would pull the skiff sideways back just like it had come, and one man would pull in the lead line and one the cork line. The man pulling the cork line would usually have the most fish to take out that were gilled (their gills stuck in the net). When they got this down to a close circle, about fifty yards of net out (this was deeper and heavier mesh net than the wings), they would do what they called bunt the net down. They'd put a spud down beside the staff to close the net up and pull the rest of the net in by hand under the spud. If they had too many fish to roll the net in, they had a big dip net they would use to bail them out.

The net went in the back of the skiff. Then there was a solid bulkhead ahead of the net and another bulkhead up close to the bow. In between is where they carried the fish.

After you took out the expenses for the gas, the money was divided into four shares. The rig got a share, and each of the three men got a share. The only exception I know to that was Cecil Sears, who had three thousand yards of net and two gas boats, and the rig got two shares. This was before they put the limit on the yardage of nets.

Now you should know what I mean by a long net rig.

Long Net Rigs at Currituck Wharf

Mr. Lou Brumsey had an old shad boat with a Model A Ford motor in it. A big black man named Amos Etheridge fished with him.

Mr. Lou had a car tire cut in half and nailed on each corner of the stern of his gas boat so the skiff wouldn't bang it. Mr. Lou was Edward "Poss"

Brumsey's daddy, and his wife was Mr. Henry Dozier's sister. Mr. Lou farmed in the summer and fished in the winter.

Mr. Earl Snowden had the first gas boat I ever remember Mr. Pat O'Neal building. The boat first had an old car engine in it, then Dr. Fondie, who Mr. Earl carried duck hunting a lot, bought him a new Chrysler Crown marine engine. The deal was he just had to take Dr. Fondie duck hunting when he wanted to go. This was the only gas boat I knew of outside the clubs that had a marine engine. Local people just couldn't afford them.

Most of the fishing was done in the winter and spring after the duck hunting season. In the early years, when Bell's Island was still a club, Mr. Earl guided there (as did Mr. Pat O'Neal and Mr. Jessie Twiford, "Hambone's" daddy). He lived on the canal bank in Coinjock right next to the Ruritan Clubhouse. He never had a car, but he had a pretty little gas boat probably about 24 feet long that he went back and forth to work in. I remember it was painted white and had a wood varnished steering wheel on the back of the cabin. It didn't have a shelter cabin. In the summertime, Mr. Earl worked for Currituck County schools painting and doing maintenance.

Mr. Bryan Snowden worked at Bell's Island, as did George Roberts. After Mr. William Steel Gray bought out the other members of the club and turned it into an Angus cattle farm, he hired Mr. Alphonso Lane full time to build fences and keep things repaired. Mr. Lane was known as one of the best carpenters in Currituck County. He was also one of the carpenters that built the Whalehead Club. Mr. Ed Sawyer was employed there, and I'm sure many more. These are just the ones I remember.

Mr. Earl Snowden and his younger brother, Charlie, started a hunting lodge in the old Snowden house on Maple Road in the '40s or early '50s. Their mother, Miss Carrie, was living when they started the lodge. I guided for them in 1956 and 1957.

Charlie Snowden had two long net rigs. Parnell Etheridge, a big black man, ran the old Tom Brumsey boat for him, and I don't remember who helped him. That boat was 32 feet long, had a good-sized cabin up forward and most of the time had a six-cylinder Chevrolet in it, hooked up straight. This was a battery boat built for Tom and Carl Brumsey by Mr. Wilton Walker for market hunting with a battery rig.

When the Snowdens first started the hunting lodge, they left from Mill Landing in Maple. Henry Doxey used to run the boat and pull seven skiffs with the guides and men across Coinjock Bay; he'd go out through the Haul Over and on out to Great Shoal, which is between Bell's Island and Swan Island. They didn't have outboard motors then. Henry would drop

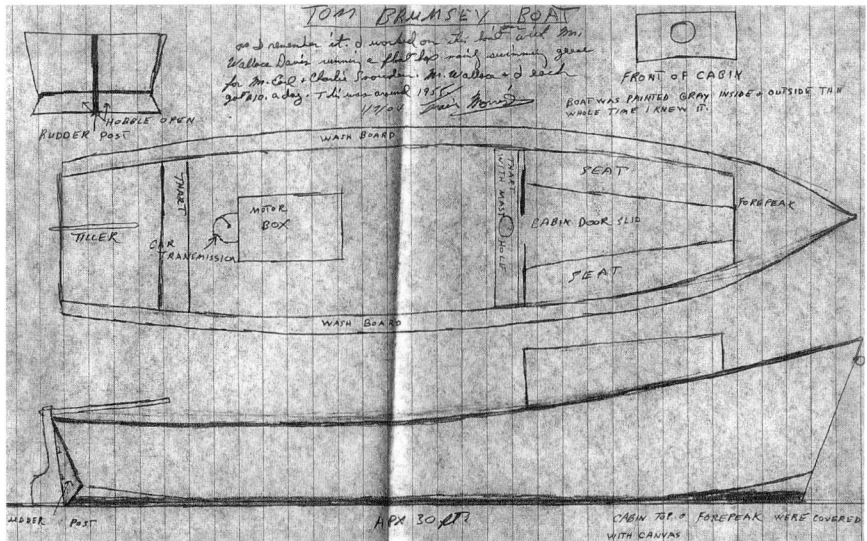

Tom Brumsey's boat. I don't know for sure who built it, but I think Mr. Wilton Walker did. When I knew the boat, Charlie Snowden owned it. At different times, different men ran it, pulling a fishing rig. In the hunting season, it was used for a float box rig. Mr. Wallace Davis and I ran it two seasons for Charlie and his brother, Mr. Earl Snowden. This was in the late 1950s. *Author's collection.*

a guide and two men off at a blind, go to the next blind and do the same. If the wind was blowing hard and a guide got out to pick up a duck and couldn't get back in, Henry would go pick him up and tow him back to his blind. In the evening, he'd go around and pick them all up and go back to Mill Landing.

This is the boat Henry was running the day a storm blew up and they had to leave the rigs. The old boat was loaded real heavy because Henry had picked up some other people that were in trouble. The guides were busy pumping and bailing. The sportsmen wanted to know where the life preservers were, and Henry told them there weren't any. When they got in, some of them called the Coast Guard. After that the Coast Guard had a special class for the guides in Currituck Sound at Griggs School. We had to go down there and get a captain's license that was just good for Currituck Sound. When my office burned in 1980, my license was in it.

This Tom Brumsey boat is the same boat Mr. Wallace Davis and I used to run a float rig for the Snowdens in during 1956 and 1957. The boat ended up at Mill Landing in Maple. Jack Privot got the boat, bailed it up and I towed it to his house at Currituck with my gas boat, *Rhonda*. I had a 442 Oldsmobile in *Rhonda* at the time, and I'm sure that is the fastest that old boat had ever been. She was leaking so bad in the bow I had to pull her fast enough to get her stem post out of the water. When we got to Jack's house, Dukie Davis and some others pulled her up right in front of his house at Currituck. This is just south of the ferry dock now. He decided it wasn't worth fixing, so he burnt her up.

Charlie Snowden had another long net rig that Jerome Doxey ran for him. I don't know who helped him. This boat was smaller than the others; it was probably about 24 feet long and not too wide. It had a deep deadrise in the bow, had a little cabin and a flathead V8 Ford motor. It was pretty swift. I don't know who built it.

Then Charlie Snowden had Mr. Wilton Walker build a boat about 20 feet long and pretty wide for Mr. Tom Brumsey to fish pound nets with. This was an open boat with no cabin. I sat on a stump and watched Mr. Wilton put the deadrise in this boat. It was stave planked. He would mark a board, chop out down the mark with a hatchet, nail it up there and caulk it.

After Mr. Tom Brumsey quit using the boat, Mr. Louis Snowden got it. He'd retired as a Commander in the Coast Guard, moved back to Maple and lived in the big two-story house on the corner of Highway 168 and Maple Road.

Pudding Rawls was married to Louise Miller, daughter of Wallace Miller Sr., and they lived in a camp at Mill Landing. Mr. Louis had a little 500-yard net that he and Pudding played with in Coinjock Bay.

One time just before duck season was coming in, Mr. Louis told Pudding to take that boat and go take inventory in Coinjock Bay. He came back and said there were three boobies (ruddy ducks) in the bay.

The next person who had that boat was Bill Snowden, and she died in his yard on Waterlily.

The first fishing rig I remember Mr. Wallace Davis having was at Currituck Wharf and was an old shad boat. He had to run her ashore every night. However deep the water was would be how deep it would be in that boat the next morning. There was no such thing as an automatic bilge pump. I can remember the bottom of that boat had so many barnacles on it there was hardly room to put a pin between them.

Mr. Wallace later got a boat that was about 25 feet long and pretty wide. I don't know where she came from, but I don't think it was built around here. The bottom was planked fore and aft and was almost flat. After Mr. Wallace quit fishing, his son Dukie ended up with it, and he and Baxter

Hand-Crafted Boats of Old Currituck

Mr. Wilton Walker built the first boat in this picture for Charlie Snowden for Mr. Tom Brumsey to fish pound nets with. The big boat you can just see part of the white cabin on was the old 33-foot Bell's Island battery boat (the boat I made my first duck hunting trip in). The boat crossways was the *Sea Lizard* and belonged to me at this time. The tide was out and it was on bottom. These boats were all up in Mill Landing because of a storm. *Author's collection.*

Williams put a straight eight Buick in it. She would run good. I don't know where the boat ended up.

When Mr. Charles Simpson and his father-in-law, Mr. Will Lee, had the store at Currituck, Mr. Charles also had a fishing rig. It was about a 25-foot flat bottom boat with pretty high sides and a cabin on it. There were no windows in the cabin. He took his son Bill and me fishing with him one day when we were just small boys. It was the first time I'd ever been fishing except with a cane pole. I remember he made a haul that day up north of Currituck off the Creekmores' farm.

I never knew Charlie Snowden to run a fishing rig himself. He was the fish buyer. One time he had a little office on the shore up at the head of the wharf at Currituck. Also at the head of the wharf was the old battery box (sink box) that Mr. Tom and Carl Brumsey had hunted with.

I remember one time Charlie had a long table made on the north side of the wharf, and it was closed in on the north side and had a shed roof over it for protection from the wind and rain. He had several black women there skinning catfish.

Fast-forward a few years. Cecil Sears, who lived in Manteo and was a full-time commercial fisherman, brought his rig up to Currituck in the 1950s.

I was married and living at Currituck at that time. I don't remember the people that fished with him, but I know he was Ralph Sears' uncle. I talked about Ralph in my third book.

Cecil had a big old house boat I'd say close to 40 feet long they lived on. She had a round stern. I think he also used it to pull one end of the net. He had another shad boat that I would say was over 32 feet with a small cabin up forward that he used to pull one end of the net. Then he had a big wide flat bottom open boat with no cabin that they called the run boat. Then there was a little skiff with an air-cooled engine they used for unhanging the net.

Cecil Sears had about 3,000 yards of net, and he would hang a boat on each end of it and pull it for half a day then come together and take it in. They would use the run boat to bring the fish in if they caught a lot while they made another haul. I don't know if this net was legal or not because at one time the net could only be 900 yards.

All three of his boats had straight eight Buicks in them and would wake up everybody in the village of Currituck when they started up mornings. I know because I was living there in the house that is beside Brumsey's Law Office. Daddy and Mama built that house in 1936. We lived there until my Granddaddy Boswood died in 1941. That house has just been turned into a restaurant named "Pass the Salt." It opened in March of 2014. In 1941, we moved to Coinjock to live with my Grandmother, and that is where I was raised. Mama and Daddy rented the house out until Frances and I moved there in 1956. We had four children born while we were living there. After Daddy died in 1972, Mama gave that house to Frances and me. We sold it and, in 1973, converted Frances' daddy's barn in Maple into a house, and that made a good place for our children to finish growing up. There was plenty of room for their friends to come visit. There was always a houseful of kids, but we had rather them be there than up and down the road. How did I get so far off the subject of boats?

The fishing that is done in Currituck Sound now is done with gill nets, pound nets or long flounder nets on a reel.

In the next section, I'm going to share some fishing stories that Bootie Spruill told me.

Bootie Spruill: Haul Net Fishing in Currituck Sound

I've known Bootie since we were in grammar school. He is five months older than me and is a native of Currituck County. We were talking at Currituck Sports, locally referred to as the "Bait Shop," and we think Bootie probably knows more about the bottom of Currituck Sound from Poplar Branch north than anybody left since "Hambone" Ambrose Twiford died. Bootie has done a lot of fishing with a haul seine from Poplar Branch to Tull's Bay.

Bootie guided sport fishermen for Caroland Farm back when we had all the milfoil (grass) and bass in Currituck Sound. We'll talk about that later when we talk about Caroland Farm.

Bootie started out fishing as a teenager when he was in high school, fishing some with Ambrose "Hambone" Twiford and with Mr. Frank Carter. He said when he was fishing with Ambrose they really caught some fish.

Bootie said he'd never forget one time they were out in the north sound near the old bombing target. "Hambone" said, "Well, we won't make but one haul, but we'll make a good one." They had about 1,200 yards of net (that was before the law cut it down to 900 yards). He ran it right straight northwest of the bombing target. He got the net all overboard about 8:00 a.m. and pulled on it until they finally got back around to the starting staff about 1:30 p.m. One time, they got hung and had to go back and unhang that (they tore a pocket out of the net that time). Ambrose was running the boat. Bootie was on the cork line, and Lynn Fulcher was on the lead line. They'd taken in about 1,000 yards of net and hadn't brought in enough fish to cover the bottom of a wire basket. They hadn't even seen a carp. Lynn stuck his lips out and said, "We ain't gonna' catch no fish today." They kept on taking in until they had just eight long stakes in the net that was still overboard (that would be about 64 feet of net left in the water). Here come one carp. Lynn said, "By God there is one in it." The next stake that came in it had so many fish in it they had to roll them out. Every once in a while, Ambrose would say, "I ain't never seen this before." His staff at the end of the net kept easing away from the boat, and he was right steady pulling back.

Bootie said, "Ambrose, yonder is the trouble."

"What's that?"

Bootie pointed and said, "Look yonder in the back of the net!" The carp looked like cordwood stacked up all around the net.

Ambrose said, "My Lord, we won't be able to carry 'em all!" They kept going along and finally got the net in, just before dark. They'd been putting all the fish in the fishing skiff, but the fishing skiff was loaded pretty good and they hadn't got the net closed up yet. Ambrose said he'd like to get it closed up if there was any way possible. He was pulling so tight it was running those perch right over the top of the cork line. Bootie said, "Hold on a minute. Let's bail some of these things." Lynn got the lead line, and Ambrose got that big dip net of his and started bailing perch, catfish and rock. They loaded the fishing skiff right there. They didn't have anywhere to put more fish, so they got the gas boat around there and loaded that up. By that time, the wind had breezed up a little bit, and it was so cold it was freezing the fish by the time the air hit 'em.

Ambrose took the gas boat load on to the fish buyer, Otto Bateman, on the Coinjock Canal. Bootie said they at least had sense enough to keep a flashlight so Ambrose could find them when he came back.

Lynn had one pair of socks on in old black rubber boots with no insulation. He was about to freeze. Bootie said he had insulated boots and clothes on and was fairing pretty good. He had a quart Thermos bottle full of coffee that he hadn't opened all day. He'd always offer Lynn some coffee and he wouldn't take it, but he took it that night. Lynn later said if it hadn't been for that coffee he'd have froze to death. It was about 9:30 p.m. or 10:00 p.m. before Ambrose ever got back out there to them. Wallace O'Neal had caught a bunch of fish and made it to Otto's ahead of him, and he had to wait for him to get unloaded before he could unload. When Ambrose got back to them, they bailed the fish out of the skiff into the gas boat, left the skiff and net that was still overboard tied up and anchored right there and came on back to Otto's.

The canal froze up that night. When a boat came through the next day and broke the ice up, they got out as far as Long Point and that was as far as they could get. They finally made it back to Mr. Pat O'Neal's shop. Elijah Tate had a gas boat that had copper on it. (You have to remember boats were wood then. No fiberglass. If you ran a wood boat through the ice, it would cut the bottom off of it just like you took a chain saw to it. Copper around the waterline would protect it.) They had a skiff on the bank. They shoved that overboard, took Elijah's gas boat and that skiff and went back out there to see if they could get the rest of the fish and the rig. They didn't completely load the fishing skiff so they would have room for the net. They finally turned the rest of the fish loose, pulled the net in and came on back. Bootie said he'd never forget how many rockfish they had. They had 1,100 pounds, and it was the week before Christmas. They got seven cents a pound for them. Bootie said if you could have gotten today's price for the fish they caught in that haul, you wouldn't have to fish anymore for a year. There were the other fish, too. They ended up selling over fourteen thousand pounds of carp.

Another time they were fishing over there around Corney Island. They had cotton net then, not nylon like it is now. This net had some holes off the lead line. Well, Lynn Fulcher was running those sticks out, and Bootie saw him when he stuck his foot in one of those holes. Lynn couldn't hear it thunder, so Bootie was shaking him and hollering, "Get your foot out! Get your foot out!" He didn't get it out in time. When that net came tight, Lynn went out of that boat like a bullet. Bootie was hollering at Ambrose, and he finally got the boat cut off. Bootie got caught in the net, and he said he was like a scissor going down through that net, but him holding that line was keeping Lynn up. Ambrose and Bootie got Lynn back in the boat, and he just said, "By God, I lost my boot!" They anchored everything just like it was and brought him on ashore to get dry clothes, and they went back over there and went on and made the haul. When they got around to where that all took place and pulled that lead line up, the boot was still wrapped in the net. At least he didn't lose his boot.

Others Bootie Fished With

Bootie said he fished with Wallace O'Neal and Lon McCloud. Lon and Bootie hung a haul seine net with the idea that they were going to run the rig. It was Archie Midgett's rig and Wallace didn't have a job, so Archie turned the rig over to him. Bootie said if they suggested making a haul in one place, Wallace would go in the opposite direction. He caught a few fish with him, but he never caught them like he did with Ambrose.

Next, Bootie and Harry Austin bought a rig from Alfred Everett and got an old skiff from Archie Midgett. Harry had a gas boat. It was all right to pull the net with, but it wouldn't carry any weight.

They made a haul over across the sound by Southeast Island one day. It was blowing a gale, and they made that haul in there and loaded down the skiff and gas boat too. They had a lot of carp, but there were also eight boxes of little fish.

They took them in to Casey Jones' dock at Waterlily and were going to sell them to Casey, but he told them he couldn't give them but two cents a pound for the carp. Otto Bateman was paying four cents at Coinjock. Bootie said, "I reckon we'll have to carry them over to Coinjock to Otto."

"It's a long ways over there," Casey said, "Just call Otto and let him come get them here." When they started picking those little fish out and it turned out to be eight boxes, Casey said, "Lord, I wish I'd known you had that many!" Bootie said he didn't have any idea it was that many little fish in there. Most of them were perch.

By this time, Harry and Bootie were both bridge tenders at Coinjock Bridge (before the high rise bridge, there was a draw bridge across the canal at Coinjock). They had to fish when they were off duty.

Harry Austin started gill netting in North River. Then Bootie and John Dennis and Johnnie Parker started fishing together. He had Blanton Saunders and Tillman Merrell fishing with him one time. William Carter and Daily Williams fished with him some.

After Bootie and Harry Austin stopped fishing together, Bootie got a flat bottom gas boat from Archie Midgett. This was the same boat that Mr. Wallace Davis, Bill Snowden and I fished for Archie when Mr. Pat first built it. Then Archie had Wallace O'Neal lengthen it out, and Archie had somebody fishing it in Dare County. Then Bootie got the boat from Archie.

Bootie kept that boat until she was giving out and needed rebuilding. He got L.M. Saunders to rebuild it, but he had to have a boat to use while this was being done.

Bootie said at one time Tillman Merrell would have sold him his gas boat for $400. He said not buying it was the biggest mistake he ever made. Now he needed it, but Tillman wouldn't sell it. Tillman said he needed it for hunting, but he did rent it to him while he was getting his boat fixed. After Bootie got his boat back, he used that as long as he fished. Then he sold it to Greg Westner, "Cuz," over on the beach. So far as I know, the boat is in Cuz's yard in Corolla now. Cuz is not fishing now. He is working for the county water department in Corolla.

Another fish story Bootie told me was one time when Blanton and William Carter were fishing with him, he was making a haul down there in that deep water, what Mr. Pat O'Neal used to call "Morgan's deep water" right off from Morgan's flats. Anyway, he said he'd stick up on the shoal—not high up but up out of the mud—and haul around in the deep water then pull around and bunt up on the hard bottom. They made the same haul three days in a row, and the last haul was bigger than the first. This was big rock they were catching.

Carp

Bootie had a man out of Winston-Salem who was buying live carp from him. He was getting twenty-five cents a pound for live carp. That is the most I've ever heard of anybody getting for carp.

Bootie made him a carp pen at Poplar Branch landing with net. I assume he towed a carp car to keep them alive until he could get them back to his pen.

The man could take about six hundred carp in his tank truck. He didn't want anything under ten pounds. A lot of time they were catching carp that weighed much more than that, and they were just averaging them. Bootie said he was getting socked on that, so he bought himself a set of scales. The man didn't like those scales too much, but he kept coming. Take a thirty- or forty-pound carp, they were really getting skinned calling it ten pounds.

The man would come get a load, and Bootie asked him when he wanted some more. The man told him to call him as soon as he got a load.

He said he got the man's truck loaded up about 8:00 a.m. Then they went out and made a haul and caught more than the man could carry. When they got back in, Bootie called the man, and he hadn't even gotten home. Bootie asked him when he was going to be able to be back. He said he couldn't come until the day after next because he had to get some sleep!

I guess that is enough long haul fishing stories for now.

Mullet Fishing

Bootie was telling me about taking Archie Midgett mullet fishing over on the beach side of the sound in Ship's and Parker's Bays. This was familiar to me because I used to mullet fish with Archie back in the mid-1950s in the same places.

Bootie said he took Archie over there one time mullet fishing. He had a linen net with four-inch mesh. The tide was fairly low. They went up there in Parker's Bay, and he put Archie overboard with one end of the net in the shallow water. Bootie said he hadn't poled out ten yards before one hit her, and he kept on going. He said they made two sets in Parker's Bay and two in Ship's Bay, and they had a little over six hundred pounds. They were big mullets to gill in four-inch net.

My First Gas Boat

Since we are talking about boats in the Currituck area, I'll tell you about my first gas boat. I think I was about fifteen years old because I didn't have a driver's license. I had $350 in my savings account that I'd saved from mowing grass and driving a tractor on the farm for my Uncle Tommy at $3 a day. Grown men got $5 a day working on the farm at the time.

I wanted a gas boat and talked Mama in to letting me spend my savings for an old flat bottom gas boat with a Model A Ford motor that Vernon Lee Creekmore had that he would sell for $350.

The Creekmores' farm was on the sound between the wharf at Currituck and the mouth of Tull's Bay, just south of the Tice farm.

One Sunday afternoon, Daddy took me and Ben Taylor up to Vernon Lee Creekmore's for me to buy the boat and bring it back to Mill Landing at Maple.

The sound was slick as a piece of glass. The boat was tied to a stake out in the sound. Vernon Lee, Ben and I went out to it in a skiff. The battery was dead, so it wouldn't start, but Vernon Lee had it rigged up so you could crank it. It had a car transmission, but you couldn't run it long without being in gear because it didn't have a water pump, just a "kicker" (this was a piece of galvanized pipe with an elbow on it facing the propeller to force water to the engine).

Vernon Lee said it would be all right—the generator would charge the battery up before we got to Maple. Ben and I took off. I thought I was really something standing back there with that tiller in my hand and that Model A just clucking. I'd never run anything larger than a 12hp, and this boat would run about 25mph wide open. When we were about a thousand yards north of Bell's Point, the generator quit ginning and the Model A quit clucking.

Travis Morris and Ben Taylor in the boat I bought from Vernon Lee Creekmore. It had a Model A Ford motor. The board on the bow of the boat is the first surf board I ever saw. Wayne Taylor made it. It had a thin wood frame covered with canvas. We used it to surf in the ocean, and we used it to pull behind this old gas boat and surf. The stern of the boat on the right of my boat is one built by Mr. Earl Ballance. It was about 18 feet long and originally had an outboard. It was launched at Mill Landing on Thanksgiving Day. Later he raised the sides and made an inboard out of it. He put a 60 flathead Ford V8 motor in it, and the engine box looked like a little cabin. It was right in the bow and was so heavy forward you had to slow it down easy or it would take a nose dive. *Author's collection.*

The water was about nine feet deep, and the shoving pole I had was twelve feet. Our only choice was to throw the anchor, pull it in and throw it again. This was mighty slow going. Jack Privott had walked down to Currituck Wharf and was looking at us with a pair of binoculars and saw our situation. He went and got Mr. Earl Snowden to take his gas boat and come and get us. He was one welcome sight.

Vernon Lee Creekmore

Before we leave Currituck, I need to tell you about another gas boat. This boat was about 25 feet long. It had a cabin with windows on both sides and in front. The back of the cabin was closed in and had a door. It had

Boating and Fishing in Old Currituck

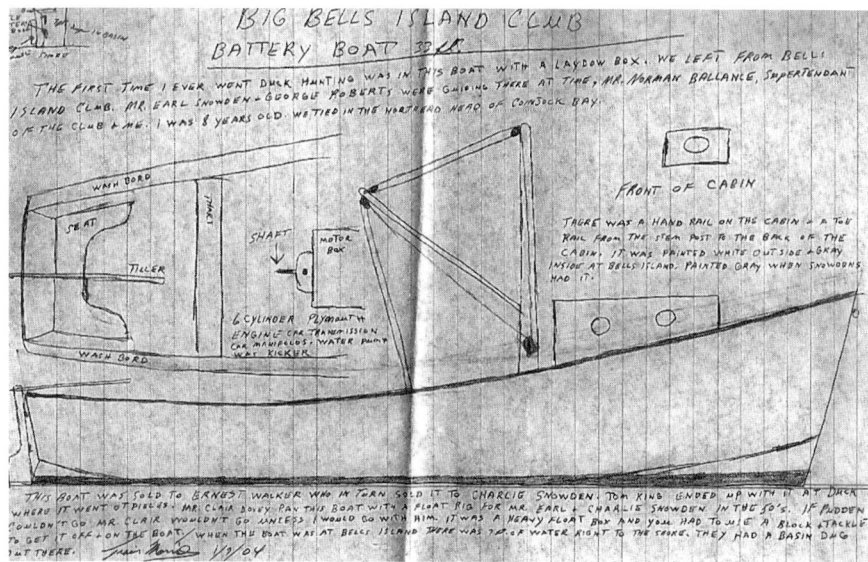

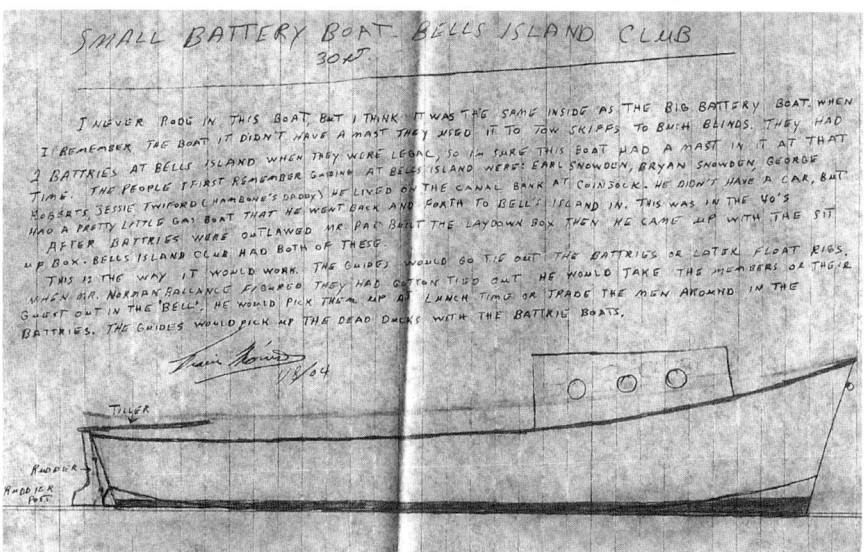

Bell's Island Club boat I drew.

a shelter cabin aft of that. Mr. Wilton Walker built it for the Tice brothers when they first came here from New York, bought a farm and started a hunting lodge.

When the Tices quit the hunting lodge, Vernon Lee Creekmore bought the boat from them. In the summertime, Vernon Lee would leave the boat at Oregon Inlet Fishing Center. Vernon Lee had two cottages in Kitty Hawk. He rented out one and kept one for his family. Baxter Williams, Fred Newbern and I fished for bluefish with him a lot. We would spend the night before at his cottage. The hot water heater was a galvanized tank on the roof—solar heat.

One night, by the time we got to Vernon Lee's cottage, the only place we could find open to eat was the Drafty Tavern on the causeway to Manteo (where Pirates Cove Marina is now). You have to remember that back then (probably the early 1960s), the beach was dead city from Labor Day to Memorial Day.

We go in the Drafty Tavern, the place was full, and who should we run into but Walton Carter and H.D. Newbern Jr. To say they were feeling no pain would be putting it mildly. The way they were talking, I was afraid we were going to get thrown out of there just because we were associating with them. I was relieved when we got out of there without getting thrown in jail.

We would eat breakfast at Sam & Omie's. The boat had a flathead Ford V8. There was no radio, and sometimes we would be out of sight of land. We would not dare cut the motor off to check the oil, afraid she might not start. When you are young, you don't see a lot of the dangers that you see when you are older. Vernon Lee later got a bigger boat, and I don't know what happened to this one, but we caught a lot of bluefish with it.

Bell's Island Club

Now we move down to Bell's Island when it was still a club. They had a harbor dredged out and bulk headed right up to the shore. It was 7 feet deep. It had a boat house that the *Bell* stayed in. The first *Bell* I remember was about 28 feet long. She was painted white outside, with gray decks and cabin top, and was gray inside. The cabin sides were varnished, and it looked like the sides of the cabin were made from this narrow bead paneling they used in houses around the turn of the century. The cabin was planked vertical and a little round to the front. The cabin had portholes on each side and the front. The back of the cabin was open and had a windshield on top of it.

There were bench seats on each side in the cabin with black leather cushions on them. There was also a seat across the stern with a black leather cushion.

Mr. Norman Ballance was superintendent of the club, and he would take the members out to the batteries after the guides had them tied out. He'd bring them in for lunch, change them around and so on.

They had two battery boats. One was 33 feet long with a high bow, a little cabin with two portholes on each side and a sliding door on the back of the cabin. There was a wide seat all the way across the boat right behind the cabin with a hole in the middle and a mast in it. The mast had a short boom with a block and tackle that was used to pick up the battery.

This boat was sold to Ernest Walker. I went to see him about buying it when I heard it was for sale, but he had just sold it to Charlie Snowden. Mr. Clara Doxey and Pudding Rawls ran it for him when the Snowdens had the hunting lodge in later years and were hunting with float box rigs.

Archie Midgett used that boat for shrimping in Croatan Sound one summer. Tom King took her to Duck. She was tied out to a stake, and that is where she died.

The other battery boat was 32 feet long, and the bow and sides were not quite as high. The cabin was longer and had three portholes on each side. This boat was sold before the big one; I don't know where she went.

Laydown and Sit-Up Boxes

After the batteries were outlawed, Mr. Pat O'Neal first came up with a laydown box that was legal. The law said you couldn't have artificial weight as the old batteries did. The laydown box Mr. Pat came up with had a deck about four feet wide and about ten feet long. It had three wings in front, one on each side and one in the back. The wings were a slat frame covered with burlap so the water could go up and down through it and not make the wing flap up and down. The wings would fold up for transporting, which was usually on a battery boat just like the batteries were carried. There was a box just like a coffin in the middle of this deck for a man to lie in. The front of the box was raised a little bit to rest your head and so you could see over your feet. The sides on the box were maybe ten inches high. There were screw eyes on the front and back wings to snap canvas-covered goose decoys to. On the deck of the box you put three geese on each side and had a strap to hold them in place made from a piece of inner tube. There were hooks made from heavy clothesline wire that were hooked to fence staples in the deck. You tied a bunch of geese around the head of the box. You would tie a large stand of ducks in a half moon or "J" at the foot of the box. Canvasback, redheads and blackheads would come right up that hole to your feet.

You could lie off in a boat, and it would look just like a raft of ducks and geese there.

The sit-up box was just as comfortable for two men as the laydown box was *un*comfortable for one man. It was built on the same principal, except the deck was not as long and was wider. The deck was made with about a two-inch frame with plywood on the top and bottom to make it watertight. It had a box just a little back of center in the frame. The foot of the box was below the water, and you were sitting level with the water. Your weight would take care of the water the foot section displaced. It would have pine bushes woven in the slats around the box. This was still a small object compared to a bush blind. It had runners the depth of the foot and was generally pulled across a big skiff for transporting. The ducks and geese were tied out in the same manner as with the sit-up box. I used ninety canvas geese and two hundred wood ducks.

Mill Landing, Maple: Charlie Snowden

The same year President Roosevelt went to the Lost Colony, 1937, Charlie Snowden had Carlos Culpepper and Oliver O'Neal build him a gas boat. They built it in the Rehoboth Baptist Church yard at Maple in the shade of the trees.

The boat was about 23 feet long. It had a flat rocking chair bottom. By that I mean the side boards were just pulled around, which made the bottom up at both ends and deep in the middle. The boat had the widest juniper boards I have ever seen. It had a high bow and narrow tumblehome stern. The cabin was open in the back except for a roll-up curtain. There were three big windows on each side of the cabin and one in front.

I first remember this boat being at Currituck Wharf. Mr. Frank Brumsey had it. I don't know if it belonged to him or if Charlie Snowden just let him use it. A black man, Gonnie Etheridge, used to run it for Mr. Frank. If Mr. Frank's nephew, Carter Lindsey, was out in the sound in the summertime

Mill Landing in Maple. The *Sea Lizard* when it belonged to Rufus Roberts. *Author's collection.*

The *Sea Lizard* after I traded Rufus Roberts and changed the name to *Edna Karl*. *Author's collection.*

with his sailboat and the wind died out, Mr. Frank would send Gonnie to take this boat and tow him in.

I next remember the boat being in the ditch beside Bell's Island Road. That ditch was deep then. Then Rufus Roberts had it at Mill Landing. He put a shelter cabin on it, closed in the back of the cabin and put a flathead

Ford V8 motor in it. Some of the cabin windows were broken out, and he had slabs of stove wood nailed over them.

I still had the boat I'd gotten from Vernon Lee at Mill Landing, and I made an even trade with that boat to Rufus Roberts. They called it the *Sea Lizard* then.

It was around 1954 when I got the boat. I fixed it up and changed the name to *Edna Karl* after Frances and Mama. Frances' first name was Karl. She was named that after Mr. Carl Brumsey, Barbara Glenn Brumsey Smith's daddy. Herbert Lange (whom I met in the Coast Guard and had as a lifelong friend) helped me put a six-cylinder Ford with a marine transmission in it.

The motor and transmission came out of a 30-foot Owens yacht that came in to the wharf at Currituck with engine trouble. It caught fire, and they turned it loose so it wouldn't burn up everything there. It drifted out toward the pier head and sank. Dukie Davis and I bought it from the insurance company for twenty-five dollars. We got it ashore, and he took one motor and I took one.

I used the *Edna Karl* for several years. In fact, in 1958, Baxter Williams and I farmed together, and that winter we used it to take sportsmen. We had my blind, and Mr. Frank Brumsey let us use his blind out on Great Shoal.

The next summer, after a big rain, I was going to the bank at Moyock, and when I went by Mill Landing, I saw she was getting low in the water. I said to myself, "I'll bail her up when I come back." When I got back, she was sunk. She had gotten down to an open seam in the side. There was no such thing as an automatic bilge pump back then. It was just a galvanized hand pump.

I got her up, brought her here to Mama's in the yard and ended up carrying her to the woods to die.

There was another boat I remember being at Mill Landing for a short while. It was probably 24 feet long, not very wide and had a round Drake Tail stern, which means it was slanted forward rather than backward. I think the boat came from the Eastern Shore, but I'm not sure about that. I think it belonged to Charlie Snowden.

I also remember a big sea sled with an inboard engine on blocks beside Bennie Welstead's Garage, which was right in front of where Carmel Walker's house is today in Maple. I heard that came from the Eastern Shore, too.

Edgar O'Neal Sr.

Edgar had an open gas boat (maybe 22 or 23 feet long) that his daddy, Clarence O'Neal, had built for him. I remember it was painted white and was flat bottom with an outboard rudder. It stayed tied up in front of the old Maple warehouse. I don't remember what kind of car engine it had in it, but it had a car transmission. I remember it had a white ball on the gearshift knob. He didn't keep it too long, and I don't know where it went.

My father-in-law, Walton Meiggs, and Edgar O'Neal were good friends. Mr. Walton got Mr. Clarence O'Neal to build him a float box. That is the one I still have today. Mr. Walton had a skiff they carried it on, but it really wasn't big enough to carry it. He and Edgar hunted with it a year or two. Then Edgar sold the boat, and the float box went in the barn until I came along.

Maple Warehouse Company

When I first remember Mill Landing, it still had the old warehouse. A group of farmers had gotten together and formed the Maple Warehouse Company. They had a channel dredged in there so freight boats could come in and pick up their produce and take it to Norfolk. These boats were 50 or 60 feet long. Mr. Ernest Walker, Mr. Will Edwards and Mr. Earl Ballance each had one. I'm sure there were more.

By the time I remember it, the warehouse was open on the south and closed in on the other three sides. It was not in use as a warehouse then. There was a man (I think his name was Parker) building row skiffs there for Harrison's Fishing Pier at Ocean View to rent out. When he died, he had one skiff he had not quite finished. I was six years old, and Daddy bought it for me for twenty-five dollars and got Buck Allen to finish it and put hobbles on it so it could be used with an outboard motor. It was tucked up in the stern for rowing. The hobbles were added on to straighten the bottom out so it wouldn't rare up with a motor. Daddy bought me a three-horse Waterwitch outboard motor to go on it. We kept it tied out to a stake in front of Aunt Flora Walker's in Maple, and he got Aubrey Walker to look after it.

Buck Allen

When I first remember Buck Allen, he lived on a house boat probably 30 some feet long that was tied up to the dock at Mill Landing. It had a round stern. As I said earlier, they'd had a channel dredged in there, and the harbor was dredged out and bulk headed. There was a dock all the way out on the north side of this harbor. This was still there in my day. He later put the boat up on dry land and still lived in it.

Later still, he built a little camp and lived in it. He had a little pen with some ducks in it. He was the cussing-ist man I've ever heard. Sometimes I didn't like to be around him. I went down there early one morning to go hunting. It was freezing cold, and the tide was high. The water had come in the duck pen and froze his ducks right in their tracks. He was pulling their feet out of the ice and cussing the Lord.

Buck had a little boat he trapped with. It had a one-cylinder Minus motor in it. Sometimes it wouldn't start, and he would get so mad with it he would unbolt it and throw it overboard. The water where he kept it was not very deep, and the bottom was hard. After he cooled off, he'd get it up, work on it and get it running again.

Henry Doxey

While we are talking about Mill Landing, I need to tell you some things Henry Doxey told me. He is eighty-nine years old at this writing in 2014.

Blanton Snowden lived in the house that Mr. Walton and Miss Birdye Meiggs (my in-laws) later owned and lived in, which is right next door to the barn that Frances and I turned into a house.

When I first remember that house, Blanton was living there, and fish nets were hanging on the front porch. Henry told me that old wharf right across the road from our house was called Chris' wharf. There are still pilings out there. That is where Blanton kept his boat. Henry said they only used about three hundred yards of net then. He said Jack Lindsey fished with Blanton.

Bill Walker was the father of Jack, Sammy, Milton, Marie Walker O'Neal and Mr. Em Sears' wife, Edith. She was "Hambone's" (Ambrose Twiford) mother-in-law.

They caught a lot of largemouth bass in Coinjock Bay, and it was legal then to sell them. Most all the fishermen then had little one-cylinder Minus Motor-Go engines in their boats. This is right after sailboats and before the car engines. We're going right far back.

There used to be a big A frame beacon just out from Mill Landing. A little ways to the east of that was a pier head, a platform. The big freight boats tied up to it. The smaller freight boats could go right in to the Maple Warehouse Company dock.

Henry told me a tugboat blew up in there one time and killed a man. It blew him clean across the road. He said then all the big boats had a Johnny house hanging over the stern. He said his family got the one off that boat.

Henry said Milton Walker told him their family had a Johnny house over the water. You could sit there and look down and see fish swimming around in the water.

Milton told Henry his daddy would make him get up early Saturday mornings to go fishing with him. He told him if he didn't get up, he weren't going to get nothing to eat because "there ain't nothing around here."

GILMAN BRUMSEY

Gilman's daddy and mother, Mr. Horace and Miss Lucy Brumsey, lived right across the road from Dodson Mathias' mother and daddy, Mr. Adrian and Miss Hilda Mathias, in Barco. They lived where the Palmer House Inn is today.

Mill Landing. The white boat is one Dodson Mathias and I bought from Gilman Brumsey and put a Model A Ford motor in. The lily pads are where Currituck Sports II is today. It is also where I caught my first bass on an artificial lure (a Johnson Silver Spoon with pork rind). *Author's collection.*

Gilman had an old flat bottom gas boat with no cabin that came from Wanchese turned upside down in his daddy's backyard. Dodson Mathias and I were in the Coast Guard at the time. He was stationed in the District Office in Norfolk. Dodson wanted to fix up a hunting rig to take his Superior Officer duck and goose hunting. We bought that boat from Gilman for thirty-five dollars and got Mr. Wilton Walker to fix it up, build a cabin on it and put an old Model A Ford motor in it. The motor came out of a plywood speedboat that had a hole knocked in the bottom. We'd bought that in Camden and hadn't gotten the hole fixed.

We carried Dodson's Superior Officer hunting in Cedar Island Bay and killed nine geese and I don't remember how many ducks. Long story short: Dodson came out of the Coast Guard a First Class Petty Officer, higher than any of the rest of us that joined the C.G. together.

C.G. Wallace

C.G. Wallace, Olie Ballance's father-in-law, was the VEPCO man here. He had an old gas boat at Mill Landing. It was probably 22 or 23 feet long, made out of thick boards and as heavy as lead. The stern was slanted forward instead of backward. It was a wide boat and had a little cabin up forward.

He got tired of messing with it and gave it to me. For some reason, I took the cabin off of it. It was probably rotten. Lange and I put that old flathead V8 Ford motor that came out of the Sea Lizard in it, and I got Pudding Rawls to run it for me taking sportsmen hunting one winter. I named it *Leaping Leana* because she bounced. I ended up giving this boat to Herbert Lange, and he carried it to his place on Little River.

Ambrose Dozier

I never knew Ambrose to be a duck hunter, but at one time, he had a nice scissors float blind rig. He had a nice gas boat about 25 feet long. The hull was built like the old battery boats but was not as long as most of them were. It had an outboard rudder, a nice cabin and shelter cabin that was closed in.

Mill Landing. The white boat is one Ambrose Dozier won in a poker game. The gray boat, *Leaping Lena*, is a boat C.G. Wallace gave me. I had Pudding Rawls run it for me one winter carrying sportsmen. Then I gave it to Herbert Lange. *Author's collection.*

I heard that Ambrose won this rig in a poker game. I know he gambled a lot. He was my mother-in-law Birdye Dozier Meiggs' brother.

At first, the boat stayed up at Currituck Wharf, and Wilson Snowden told me Gus Morse fished with it some. When I took a picture of it, the boat was at Mill Landing in Maple. It didn't stay there too long. I don't know where it went.

COINJOCK: PAT O'NEAL

Henry Doxey told me that Mr. Pat O'Neal told him that George Washington Creef (who invented the shad boat) built a boat for him one time. He said Mr. Pat went to Manteo and lived with Mr. Creef while the boat was being built. After it was finished, they put a motor in it, and he brought it home. Newton Hampton said Mr. Pat had told him the same story.

The first personal boat I remember Mr. Pat owning was about 35 feet long and almost as deep in the stern as it was in the bow. It had a little tumblehome in the stern, and the stern had a little round, but not like you think of a round stern boat. And the stern was pretty straight up and down. It had a pretty long forward cabin with several windows, not portholes.

Left: Patrick Henry O'Neal (1897–1972). My first job was working for Mr. Pat. That was when I got my Social Security number. I was not a boat builder, but I could scrape and paint. *From* Heritage of Currituck County, North Carolina, 1985.

Below: Mr. Pat's personal boat that he carried sportsmen in and commercial fished with as best I can remember it. On the right-hand side in the back of the cabin he had a closed-in head so he could take women. *Drawn by author.*

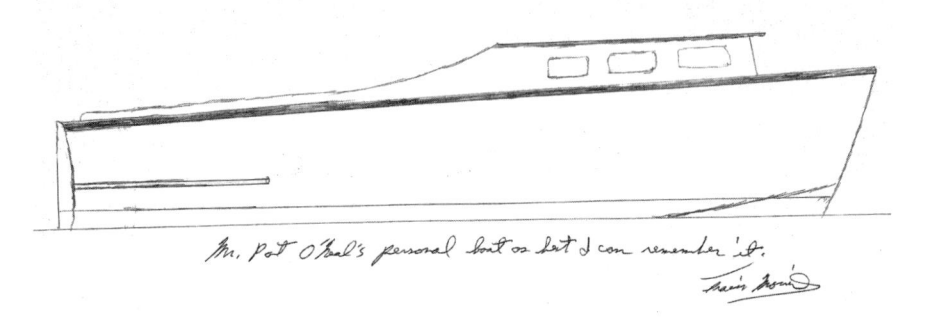

Although you couldn't stand up in the cabin, there was an enclosed head (commode). It did not have a shelter cabin, and I don't remember what kind of motor it had in it.

When he had this boat, he carried sportsmen in the winter and fished with a long net after hunting season. In the summer he built boats. I think this must be the boat that Mr. Elijah Tate will tell you Mr. Pat built for himself. I can't remember what happened to the boat, and since Hambone's dead, there is nobody left to ask. You see that's why I'm writing about these old boats: when I'm gone, the knowledge of most of these old boats is gone. I got off on another tangent. Back to the story.

The first concave tunnel boat Mr. Pat O'Neal built. Mr. Carl White got him to build it for Pine Island Club. *Elizabeth Tate.*

The second concave tunnel boat Mr. Pat O'Neal built. He built it for Bell's Island Club in 1948. The boat had a spray hood with no cabin. It was later owned by Piney Island Club; they changed the name to *Mother Goose*. It was later owned by me, and I gave it to the Whalehead Preservation Trust. It is on the National Register of Historic Boats. *Author's collection.*

Boats that I can remember Mr. Pat building: I told you earlier the first boat I remember him building was for Mr. Earl Snowden. The next boats are not necessarily in the order he built them.

The first concave tunnel boat he built was for Mr. Carl White for Pine Island. It was about 25 feet long with a flathead Chrysler Crown marine engine. I think it was 115hp. There was no cabin, but it had a spray hood. Mr. Pat wanted to keep them light so they would run fast.

The next one was just like it except this one had a commode up forward for Mrs. Gray. Mr. Norman Ballance had him build it for Mr. William Steel Gray, who owned Bell's Island. He was chairman of Manufacturers Hanover Bank and Trust Company in New York City, among other things.

The Ferrell brothers got this boat when they bought Bell's Island. They ended up putting a cabin and shelter cabin on it. Then Piney Island Club got it, and I ended up with it and gave it to the Whalehead Preservation Trust. It is registered in the Library of Congress on the National Register of Historic Boats.

He built another one of these boats for Frank Penn for Monkey Island. That boat is just like Mr. Pat built it, and at present it is under my shelter and belongs to the Whalehead Preservation Trust. This boat does not have as much deadrise as the others. He wanted it to go in real shallow water.

Mr. Pat built a little speedboat for Mr. Orville Woodhouse about 20 feet long with a three-inch step in it. This was sometime in the 1940s. He named it the *Phyllis Ray* after one of his daughters. The boat had a flathead 150hp Fireball Gray marine engine with two carburetors and would run 54mph. That is the fastest boat I ever rode in. A lot of the fellows were racing in Dowdy's Bay back then.

Mr. Woodhouse also used the boat to take hunters from his dock on Neal's Creek to marsh guard camps at Brant Island, where a guide would take them in a skiff to a blind in a pond, or to the guard camp at Burris. At the time, Mr. Woodhouse was leasing the Narrows Island and Burris marsh.

Mr. Pat built a boat for himself. He also built the cabin on this one. Before he ever used it, John Jr. Wright talked him into selling it to Mr. Chatham for Dew's Island Club. This was the *Mildew*, which is still at Dew's Island.

Then Mr. Woodhouse got Mr. Pat to build him one of those concave tunnel boats about 23 feet long in 1952. Billy Corbell was working at Mr. Pat's shop at the time, and he built the cabin and shelter cabin on it. Mr. Pat took the speedboat in on trade. When I was working at Mr. Pat's shop, I painted the boat. He was going to fix it up but never did. J.W. Saunders

The *Phyllis Ray*. The fastest ride I ever had in a boat was in this boat. They said it would run 54mph. It had a flathead Gray Marine Fireball engine with twin updraft carburetors. *Larry Woodhouse.*

This picture was taken after the *Mildew* had been rebuilt with a Billy Corbell cabin. *Tom & Jerry* is the other boat in the picture at Wright Brothers landing at Deep Creek in Jarvisburg. *Author's collection.*

ended up with it and rebuilt it for a crab boat I think. The last I heard of the boat, it was in Ralph Aydlett's yard on the canal bank.

Mr. Woodhouse had a boathouse at Neal's Creek that he kept his boats in. Billy Corbell built the cabin on this boat. In later years, the cabin rotted, as did the stem post. Burwell Beasley put a straight stem post in the boat and just a plain cabin with no windows. Bill Tate got it next, then he sold it to Dennis Anderson of Grave Digger fame, and I don't know what happened to it from there.

Mr. Pat made a boat just like the one he made for Mr. Woodhouse for Swan Island Club. That one may have been a foot longer; Billy Corbell also made the cabin on this boat. I don't know what ever happened to that boat.

When Archie Midgett, Mr. Pat's brother-in-law, retired from going on a boat, he came back to Coinjock and lived with Mr. Pat and Miss Madeleine. He got Mr. Pat to build him two flat bottom skiffs just alike about 22 or 23 feet long. He put a motor in one and used it for a gas boat. The other one he used for a big fishing skiff. Mr. Wallace Davis was the captain, Bill Snowden pulled cork line and I pulled the lead line. We fished this rig one winter. Booty Spruill ended up with that rig. We've already talked about that.

The last gas boat Mr. Pat had for himself was a little shad boat. I don't think it was over 20 feet long. He had a little four-cylinder Gray marine engine in it. I think it was about 40hp. I don't know who built that boat.

Newton Hampton wanted to build a gas boat. Mr. Pat helped Newton set the boat up in Mr. Pat's shop. It was about 24 or 25 feet. This boat was deadrise with a concave tunnel. The sides were not tumblehomed in the stern; they were flared out. He had a cabin on it with no windows. He had the deck raised up so it would be self-bailing. You stepped down to get in the cabin, and there was no shelter cabin. The engine was a 283 Chevrolet converted to Chris Craft marine engine. He bought that from Casey Jones, who took it out of the big shad boat he'd sold to "Hambone."

Mr. Pat built a boat for John Wood Foreman almost just like the *Mildew*. He kept it at the farm he owned at the North end of Narrow Shore. Lofton "Preacher" Riddick lived in the house there. Roberts Brothers in Shawboro leased the farm and had a hog operation there. John Wood had a float rig that "Preacher" ran every day in the hunting season. One day he took people for John Wood and the next day for the Roberts brothers. He usually would tie the float box in Peter's Quarter, and if he had four men, he'd put two in a dog box, as "Hambone" called it (this was a duck blind with no skiffway). This was on the south end of Green Lump Shoal. He could wait on both rigs with the gas boat that way.

John Wood Foreman's boat, built by Mr. Pat O'Neal in 1948. The original cabin on the *Mildew* was just like the one on this boat. *Left to right, in boat*: Faye Jones, Bobby Miller, Elsie Jean Jackson and Kelly Miller. *Janet Riddick Sawyer.*

People I know of that helped "Preacher" with that rig were: Vance Aydlett Sr., Bootie Spruill, Earl Baum, Newton Hampton and I'm sure more that I don't know about or remember.

I got Mr. Pat to put a new shelter cabin on *Rhonda*. I didn't have much money, so I worked it out painting boats for him. I had painted this Foreman boat, and Mr. Pat and I were taking it back to Narrow Shore. We were going down the ditch beside Waterlily road, and Mr. Pat always ran everything wide open. The steering cable broke, and she came right up beside of Waterlily road. Floyd Simmons was working with me at the time on the farm. I got a ride home with somebody that came along and got Floyd and an old Case tractor I had, and we got her pushed back overboard.

When John Wood quit using the boat, Wayne Penn Twiford had it for a little while. Then he sold it to Levie Bunch Jr., and so far as I know, it is under his shed on the west side of Coinjock Bridge at this writing.

Mr. Pat helped John Jr. Wright and Fluff Parker set up two gas boats just alike in John Jr.'s boathouse at Deep Creek. These were built for the Chathams and Hanes. One was named the *Helen C*. It made the rounds. Ernie Bowden owned it at one time. Levie Bunch Jr. owns it as of this writing, and it is under his shed west of Coinjock Bridge.

I don't remember the original name of the other boat, but Tommy and Jerry Wright ended up with it, and it is now named *Tom & Jerry*. Billy Corbell

Bill Riddick's boat sitting, rotting, at Wright Brothers landing at Deep Creek in Jarvisburg. *Author's collection.*

built the cabin on that boat. Somebody from the Hanes Company came down and built the cabin on the *Helen C.*

About the same time he was setting up these boats, Mr. Pat helped Bill Riddick set up a boat in a shed beside Miss Mattie Wright's house. This boat did not have a tunnel in it and was pretty high sided in the stern. In addition to duck hunting, he wanted to rockfish with it in Albemarle Sound. This boat is now sitting on blocks at Tommy and Jerry Wright's landing at Deep Creek, rotting. This is not Deep Creek, Virginia. It is behind the Cotton Gin.

Elijah Tate

I've told you what I personally know about Mr. Pat's boat building, but you need to hear about boat building in Currituck County from Mr. Elijah Tate, who was a generation older than me. Some of it will be a repeat of what I've told you, but you need to get his version. The following is a direct quote from what he told his wife, Elizabeth, to go in the book *Heritage of Currituck County North Carolina, 1985*:

Currituck County is a narrow strip of land practically surrounded by water and, before 1918, extended almost to Kill Devil Hills; therefore, Kitty Hawk was part of Currituck County. This is where I was born in 1902 but moved to Martin's Point two or three years later.

Martin's Point was a 600 acre plantation of timber and farmland situated on Martins Point Creek. It was owned by Miss Hannah Lyons of Asbury Park, N.J., who purchased it from the Hodges Gallop heir—Willis Gallop. Hodges Gallop started this plantation in the early 1800s and at one time had 100 slaves.

The Gallops built 3 schooners near the head of this creek and they were used for trade in the West Indies, and as far south as Martinque and St. Kitts. There were plenty of oak and pine trees suitable for ship building on this property and an abundance of slave labor. I can show you today where those vessels were launched. I can also show you the trenches where the planks were cut with a cross-cut saw to be used for the timbers. One man stood in the trench and one man above. The railways are also recognizable where the ships were pulled up and repaired. They were registered as being built in Kitty Hawk, as all that section of the beach was known at that time.

Willis Gallop died before the Civil War and his son concealed the ships in Martin's Point Creek, but the Federals found out they were there. One of the ships was loaded with nails, slated for the West Indies. Mr. Gallop learned they were coming to confiscate them and started to move them to Hog Quarter Creek, which was on the Powell's Point side of the sound. He was caught before arriving at his destination and I do not remember what happened then. This information came through my father from the Captain of the vessel's son, who has been dead for many years.

My great uncle had a schooner built at Kitty Hawk. It was used after the Civil War for carrying freight and passengers on the rivers and sounds of that section of the country. After his death, my father came in possession of it. He kept it as long as it was useful and the rotted hull lies on the bottom of Kitty Hawk Bay. It is covered with mud and sand of course, but I believe I know its location well enough that today I can stick a pike pole in its bottom.

Also built in Kitty Hawk was Captain Harris Midgett's "Low Willis" which ran from Norfolk to all points south; engaged in the same kind of trade available at that time—freight, passengers, fish, and general cargo. Her remains are also in Kitty Hawk Bay. He had another one built to take her place. The "Van Duzon." To my knowledge, built by John Roley in about 1907 and instead of sails it was powered by a Continental kerosene engine of 20 hp. It could make a round trip to Elizabeth City and return on 45 cents worth of kerosene. I am not positive she was built in Kitty Hawk, but I know she was finished up and the motor installed there.

John Roley was quite a boat builder. His home was on Roanoke Island, but he'd go anywhere to build a boat. That was his trade. My father hired him to come to Martin's Point and build one for him. I was three years old at the time and I just barely remember it being built. It was equipped with two hot head palmer engines which did not prove successful and it was discarded before too long.

After this unsuccessful venture, Dad went to the Sportsmen's Boat Show at Madison Square Garden and came back to Martin's Point with a set of plans and a model of what he wanted. He again contacted Mr. Roley and had him come to our home and build this boat according to the plans he brought from New York. It was a V bottom design, 45 X 10 feet with a 4 cylinder 32 horsepower 1906 standard gasoline engine. When the keel of this boat was set up, Mr. Roley walked up to our house which was about 200 yards from the boat shop, took me by the hand and led me down to the new keel. He gave me a nail and a hammer and said, "now son, I want you to drive the first nail in this boat." I was about 4 years old, and this was my first awareness of boats and what they meant to my family. We named her "Dixie" and from 1906–1914, she was the fastest boat in Eastern North Carolina. She was never passed by any size boat up to that time and the top speed was 18 m.p.h.

These were some of the early boats I have heard about and remember, but there have been hundreds built here in the county. The geographical location makes it practically a necessity for the residents to own boats. Their livelihoods depend on the water and farming, as we have never had much industry to add to the economy.

The only man that I know of in Currituck County to build Shad boats was Wallace O'Neil, Sr. of Aydlett. He built the prettiest and "sailing-est" Shad Boat I think was ever made. They all came in the 22–32 ft. category and there was very little variation in their shapes. These were "Sprit Sail" boats, which in later years were changed to gasoline powered. How many he built I don't know, but I bought one of them a long time ago, after someone else had used it for years. It was a good handling boat and I was sorry to see it wear out.

Allen Hayman was born in Elizabeth City, but later moved to Point Harbor and set up a boat shop there. His father was a good boat builder and he followed in his footsteps. He stayed in business for about twenty years and built any type from row skiffs to millionaires' yachts from 14 to 65 feet. Some were built for sport fishing and they were equipped as well as any boat of that type could be. He is still living, but his building days are in the past.

Joe Hayman was my neighbor. He built boats when machinery wasn't available. It had to be done by hand. He used the very best materials and his craftsmanship was outstanding. He built out-board boats, skiffs, fishing and duck hunting boats. He was slow but his work was neat and his boats had dry bottoms. He kept this work up until about fifteen or twenty years ago and then he started making duck and goose decoys. I still have numerous duck and goose heads he carved for me in his later years. [My grandson Chandler Sawyer said he thought a Joe Hayman ruddy duck had sold for $10,000 or $11,000, but he was not sure. A Joe Hayman canvas goose will bring $300 to $350.—TM]

Levy Perry was also a good boat builder. In fact he was an all-around expert carpenter. He could build caskets, furniture, boats, houses and a lot of different ornamental things. Whenever my father needed any repair work or a boat remodeled, he always sent for Levy Perry.

Riley Beasley grew up near Corolla where he built numerous small boats for fishing and hunting. These were all shallow draft boats. He moved to Coinjock sometime in the '20s and was my neighbor as long as he lived. He built a 30 ft. deadrise for my brother-in-law and one for me. A man in Norfolk had him build a 45 ft. yacht and install a 225 h.p. engine. It was launched here in the canal and when tested out found out to be capable of 30 m.p.h. The owner was very pleased and took it to Norfolk to have the super-structure finished up there. I think this was the last boat Riley ever built, as his health was failing at that time.

Bob Morse of Churches [sic] Island was a builder of boats and decoys. All his work was done with hand tools from 1912 to 1960. All his boats were in the hunting and fishing category, except two. One was built as a tanker to carry fuel oil to the different hunting clubs. It was 40 or 45 feet long and 12 feet wide—named "Matchless." He had the reputation of building the fastest boats with a 4 h.p. engine. He had one that would run 12 m.p.h. He also built one for Henry Hampton, Sr. It was about 26 ft. long and built light weight for racing purposes. It was powered by a Roberts Motor of 3 cycles. The speed was never determined because it was used in a rough sea and a plank came off and it went to the bottom. He also was good with a pocket knife and spent a lot of his spare time whittling decoys. [One of his ruddy ducks has been sold for $42,500.—TM]

I have known Pat O'Neal ever since I can remember. He was typically Irish, short in stature, but long in wit and personality. He had a boat shop here on the canal bank that was the gathering place for old and young. His family was his first love and boats came next. You could find him just about every day in the week in his shop. In the summertime the children of the neighborhood used the boat basin for a swimming hole and the bank for hot-dog roasts. Most of the kids in Coinjock learned to swim right there under Pat's watchful eye. He used his boats to carry neighbors to the beach and on picnics and camping trips. Sometimes a net was taken along and the fish caught and cooked on the shore. There was always something going on down at Pat's shop. He built many boats of 25 ft. and he built one for his own use that was 35 feet. This was the boat he used to carry a sink box for duck hunting when sink boxes were legal. It was sturdy and well-built and lasted for years and the name? "Little Pat."

He was the first man to build a successful tunnel-boat for shallow water, and John Wright, Jr. has three of them. Swan Island has one and I believe there is still one at Poyner's Hill and Dew's Island. Practically all his boats were V bottomed, and tunneled for shallow draft. He had a style no one seemed to be able to copy and they were good looking boats. Once a man in Florida commissioned him to build a 50 ft. yacht. After he came up here and approved of it he asked Pat to deliver it to him at his Marina in Florida. He reluctantly agreed, but made the trip in good time and the owner of the boat sent him back home by plane. I never heard a complaint on any of Pat's work. He was a good carpenter, a good citizen, and a good friend.

He had a brother, Louis, who was good also. He never built boats as a profession, but he could build just as pretty a boat as you'd want to see, and what he could do with a block of wood and a pocket knife was amazing. The birds and animals he fashioned were something to remember. I saw him take a juniper stump and a hatchet and chop out a replica of a Chesapeake retriever that looked so natural you'd swear he'd bark at you. I miss Pat and Lewis. They had a smile and a joke for everybody and it will take a longtime to dim the smile of their personalities.

Wilton Walker, Sr. has his boat shop at what is known as the "Launch." This was quite a way from where I live so I didn't get to see Wilton very often, or many of his boats. There is one boat outstanding in my mind that he built for Mr. Thurston in Norfolk. If I remember correctly it was 50 ft. long and 12 ft. wide with a V bottom. It was complete in all detail and turned out to be a very beautiful job. This was built in the '20s or '30s and I think it is still in service. Mr. Walker had planers, band-saws, and joiners, which made his work go much faster than the hand tools. He knew the boat-building trade and took pride and pleasure in his work. As he grew older, he had to slow down, and finally he made only shoving paddles. I'm still using three of the last ones he made.

Last but not least, I want to mention the Dowdy Brothers of Grandy—Richard and Lawrence—they were both good boat builders. They inherited their love for woodworking from their Pennsylvania Dutch grandparents so I've been told.

When Richard was in the Coast Guard at Caffey's Inlet, he made a boat for himself in order to go back and forth across Currituck Sound. It was about 20–22 ft. long made of juniper and had a motor-go engine. He also built a sailing skiff for his daughter which was equipped with a blue and white sail made of bed ticking. He retired from the Coast Guard in 1940 and then began building boats on a full-time basis. Most of them had tunnel bottoms for shallow water and were used by hunters and fishermen. He also built shoving pole skiffs for anyone who wanted them, but the most controversial boat he ever built was for a Navy man stationed at Poyner's Hill. He was from Florida and wanted an air-boat like they used on the lakes down there. Mr. Dowdy had never seen one and had no idea of how to build it, but with a lot of instructions and some trial and error he built what the man wanted and it operated very successfully. When he was transferred from Poyner's Hill he took the boat home with him.

Lawrence built boats also. Mostly small gas boats with 2.5 to 4 h.p. engines. Bob Morse of Churches Island [sic] was building the same type at the same time, so he and Lawrence had a contest as to who could build the fastest boat with a 4 h.p. Motor-Go engine. I don't remember the winner, but they made speed up to 12 m.p.h. or more, and that was really breezing along at that time.

Lawrence built a lot of boats and as time went on motors got more powerful and the boats were built larger and on different lines. Some of the last of his boats ran as fast as 50 m.p.h.

These are just a few of the boats built in Currituck. If you look at the records it seems that every landing in the county had a shop for this purpose. There were three vessels built right here on the Coinjock Canal bank. They were 65 ft. long—the Jamie, Alice Lorainne, and Emily Marguerite. They were used for hauling barrel staves from Farmers Manufacturing Company to Points North. The Jamie and Emily Marguerite also hauled freight, lumber, and shingles from Mill Tail Creek to points on the Alligator River and Albemarle Sound. The Jamie, later named the Prophet, left Newport

News for Norfolk on her last trip. The fog was thick and she hit the rocks at the mouth of the Naval Base and ended up a total loss. The Alice left Mill Tail Creek loaded with lumber and sank in a thunderstorm. I haven't heard of the Emily Marguerite in years, but I imagine she's gone the way of all old boats.

This is just a few of the builders and the boats they made here in Currituck. I am sure there are many, many more as there will always be boats used here and someone will be sure to build them.

—*Elijah Tate*

When I was running my float box rig carrying sportsmen in the 1960s, Mr. Elijah Tate had a float rig, as did Mr. Norman Ballance (Earl Ballance's brother) at Bell's Island. We'd talk on the phone most every night to see where the ducks were. We were all three hunting in different areas of the sound. Mr. Elijah and I kept our boats at Jones' Dock in Waterlily. Mr. Norman left from Bell's Island.

Mr. Elijah's boat was tied right at the head of the dock on the right side. He'd drive up there with his pickup and get out with his gun and his lunch box, and anybody with him better have their gear, too, because he was going to untie that boat, jump in, hit the starter and go. The six-cylinder Ford motor was hooked up straight. He was most likely heading to the Gull Rock. You had to be fast to beat him there.

The next boat I can think of in Coinjock belonged to Willard Fulcher. He got it from Raynard Collins. At one time, Collins had two six-cylinder Chevrolet motors in it, and I think he used it for shrimping. This boat was at least 30 feet long but was not a shad boat.

Oscar Roberts had a flat bottom gas boat with a cabin on it that he built while he was working for Mr. Pat O'Neal. I don't know what happened to that boat.

When Burwell Beasley was living in Virginia, he built a nice gas boat about 25 feet long and good and wide. It had a cabin and shelter cabin on it. There was a little step down to go in the forward cabin. I think he sold it to Raynard Collins before he put an engine in it. It had a jet drive in it that was not successful. It stayed stopped up with grass. Collins sold it to Atlantic Research, and they used it to take people back and forth from Waterlily to the Whalehead Club when they owned Whalehead Club. When Atlantic Research left, Gene and Shirley Austin were working there, and they were kept on as caretakers. Gene ended up with the boat. At that time, it had a Buick engine in it.

Before there were any roads to Corolla, Gene and Shirley kept a car at Jones' Dock in Waterlily and an old Jeep in Corolla. They boarded their three girls, Cathy, Jennie and Patsy, with Woodrow Whitson in the winter during the week to go to school, and would take them back to Corolla on weekends. This boat was their main means of transportation before the road up the beach. The Buick wore out, and Gene put a Mercruiser in it. Gene later sold the boat to Wilson Snowden, who took the shelter cabin off it, and as of this writing, the boat is in Wilson's shed at Currituck. His wife, Barbara, got the boat on the National Register of Historic Boats the same time she got the Slick boat and the *Mother Goose* on the register.

Riley Beasley

Riley Beasley lived along the canal bank west of where Coinjock Marina is today. He built right many gas boats (Grissie Barco helped him). I'll tell you about the ones I know about.

He built a gas boat about 25 feet long with a cabin and shelter cabin for Mr. J.I. Hayman, probably in the late 1940s. Mr. Hayman would rockfish with it, then he'd take it up to Currituck Wharf during hunting season. He and Mr. Frank Brumsey would use it to tow a skiff out to Mr. Frank's blind on Great Shoal.

One September when we had a hurricane, the boat was tied up at Mr. Pat O'Neal's shop on the canal in Coinjock, and a barge got loose and messed it up.

Mr. Hayman sold the boat to Cecil Whitson, who housed it taking hunters and fishermen as long as he lived. I think Levie Bunch Jr. got it from Mrs. Whitson and gave it to the Maritime Museum in Beaufort, North Carolina. The last I knew, the boat was outside and hadn't been restored.

Riley Beasley built another boat just like that for Mark Doxey except it didn't have a shelter cabin. It just had a windshield. Mr. Mark took Daddy and me duck hunting in it one day. I don't know what ever happened to that boat.

The third boat I remember was just like Mr. Mark Doxey's, and he built it for Bill Snowden. The only difference was it had horn frames in the bow (the frames flared out). Bill told me that was the only gas boat Riley Beasley built with horn frames.

He built an open boat about 22 or 23 feet long for either Will or Clem Ross. This boat had a deep deadrise, was not too wide, was tumblehome in

Hand-Crafted Boats of Old Currituck

The first boat in the picture was Hambone's shad boat. He had traded that boat to Levie Bunch Jr. for a double-ended fiberglass boat. Levie gave it to the museum in Beaufort, North Carolina, with the understanding they would restore it. When they did nothing to it, he took it back and gave it to the Whalehead Preservation Trust, who had it restored. The second boat in the picture was built in Coinjock by Riley Beasley for J.I. Hayman. Later it was sold to Cecil Whitson, then to Levie Bunch Jr., who gave it to the museum in Beaufort, North Carolina. *Wilson Snowden.*

Bill Snowden coming out from the Whalehead Club in the 1950s. Riley Beasley built this boat for him. This picture was right after the marsh had been filled in at Whalehead Club for the airstrip. *Zoroda Snowden.*

the stern and had a spray hood and Model A Ford motor. The last time I saw the boat it was in the ditch on the north side of Waterlily Road right by Piney Island Road.

To my knowledge, the last gas boat he built was for his brother, Elwood Beasley. The boat was 24 feet long, had a high bow and low tumblehome stern. It had wide washboards and was about a foot and a half decked over the stern. It had a spray hood on it and had a six-cylinder Chevrolet engine hooked up straight; it would run 33mph. This boat had "Betty Ann" painted on the stern. Elwood Beasley kept it tied to a stake in Currituck Sound in front of his house on Church's Island (Waterlily). It was the fastest boat on the Island until Mr. Pat O'Neal built a flat bottom boat for Bill Twiford that was faster. Then Mr. Beasley took the boat to Grissie Barco and got him to put a cabin and little shelter cabin on it.

I used to ride over to Waterlily and see that boat tied out to a stake, and I admired it so much and thought how I would like to have it. When Elwood Beasley died, the boat was put in the ditch beside the road to Waterlily. I saw it advertised in the *Daily Advance* for $1,000. At the time, that was way out of my reach. It sat there about a year, and then one night I saw it in the paper for $400. I had just picked my soybeans and went right over to Waterlily and gave Mrs. Beasley $400 for the boat.

The next day, I got Joe Ringer to go with me to get it started. We put a new battery and some fresh gas in it and got it running. I carried it to Mill Landing in Maple. This was around 1963. I changed the name from *Betty Ann* to *Rhonda*, for my youngest daughter. I kept the boat at Maple for about a year, then I rented dock space from Mr. Casey Jones at Waterlily and kept it there as long as I had the boat.

I soon got Mr. Pat to put a bigger shelter cabin on it, and I had side curtains and a back curtain made for it. The Chevrolet was hooked up straight, and when I first went to Mr. Casey's, he made me tie out to the end of the dock. He was afraid I'd tear up something. When he found out I could handle the boat, I worked my way about halfway up the dock.

Next I put a 442 Oldsmobile hooked up straight in the boat, and he sent me right back to the end of the dock. I later put Bar water-cooled manifolds and a marine transmission on the motor and got my place up to the head of the dock on the south side, where I kept it as long as I had the boat. The exception was when Elijah Tate came over sometimes during hunting season; I then had to move one boat length out. He outranked me.

I used this boat to hunt with myself with my float rig to take my friends. "Hambone" and I used it to take sportsmen for many years. The only people I ever trusted to run the boat without me in it were "Hambone" and my son, Walton.

When I started developing Corolla Village, I used this boat to take my clients back and forth to Corolla. The four years I ran Monkey Island Club, I used the boat to take people back and forth to the island and to the blinds on the beach. "Hambone" brought the guides to work every morning in it, and I could always count on him being there, regardless of the weather. After the Oldsmobile, I went through two 318 Chrysler marine engines.

The following two stories I have told in one of my earlier books. I don't remember which one, but my boat *Rhonda* was so good to me on those bad nights I just wanted to tell them again. "Hambone" and I were in the sound two real bad nights in this boat looking for people. One summer when I was running Monkey Island, I had my sailboat out there. One afternoon my son, Walton; his girlfriend, Donna Williams; Norman Tadlock; and his girlfriend, Lynn Sawyer, were out in the sailboat and a storm came up. John LaRoke was the caretaker out there at the time. It was dark when he called me and said they hadn't come in.

I went and got "Hambone" to go with me in *Rhonda*. It was blowing so hard I knew if the sailboat had turned over I'd never see them again because they couldn't have held on to it.

The wind was blowing hard northwest. I had a strong spotlight on *Rhonda*. We went up north of Ship's Bay and were working our way on around the marsh to Parker's Bay with the spotlight.

What had happened was the mast had broken in the sailboat, and they managed to steer it to Rolland Twiford's blind, which was northeast of Mary Island. They had managed to get the boat in the skiffway. When they saw us coming around the marsh with the spotlight, they let the white sailboat about halfway out of the skiffway so we could pick it up with the spotlight.

When "Hambone" and I got out to the point of Little Raccoon Island, we shined the light out toward Rolland's blind and picked up the sailboat. I can't explain the relief I had when I saw that sailboat.

In the meantime, Frances had called the Coast Guard. We picked up the kids and took the sailboat in tow. The kids just had bathing suits and life jackets on and were about to freeze. They were glad to get in the cabin of *Rhonda*.

When we got to Monkey Island, the Coast Guard boys were tied up to the dock there waiting for morning. They had an inflatable boat and didn't know where to go. I don't blame them because they were not familiar with the waters.

We secured the sailboat at Monkey Island and took the kids on back to Waterlily. I think the Coast Guard boys spent the night at Monkey Island, and I don't blame them; it was one bad night.

Next Bad Night in the Sound

Mr. Charles Simpson was helping me guide at Monkey Island. After the hunting season one year, he wanted to know if he could trap the marsh, and I told him he could.

One slick, calm day just about night, Miss Katherine (Mr. Charles' wife) called me and said Charles hadn't come in and asked if I'd go look for him. I told her I would. She said their son, Billy, wanted to go with me. I told her that would be fine. My son, Walton, was living with us then, so I took him, stopped and picked up Billy. We went up to "Hambone's" house to see if he'd go with me, and as always, he said, "Just let me get my rain gear."

Mr. Charles had a skiff with a 50hp Mercury outboard motor. We figured he had broken down and gone to a duck blind. It was so foggy you could hardly see the bow of the boat, and it was just about dark. I had to go to Monkey Island first as I had a compass reading to there. From there, I had compass readings to the blinds. There was no such thing as GPS then.

Miss Katherine had called the Coast Guard right after she called me. They sent boys up from Oregon Inlet Coast Guard Station with an inflatable boat with an outboard motor. We had been to many of the blinds and couldn't find him. The wind came up out of the southeast and was blowing a gale. We anchored in the lee of Raccoon Island, and the Coast Guard boys found us and came up and tied up to us. About midnight we decided to go to Monkey Island.

The Coast Guard boys were following me. Just about halfway between the beach and Monkey Island, *Rhonda* took a sea over her stern quarter. I had never had anything like that happen before. When we got to the island at the entrance to the boat basin, I told Walt to keep the spotlight on the entrance because we had one shot. I had one hand on the steering wheel and one on the throttle. If I missed, we'd be on the bulkhead, and that would be the end of the boat. We made it, and the Coast Guard boys were right behind us. They had a radio, and the Coast Guard station at Coinjock had clocked the wind at 93mph. I had a wind gauge at home that registered to 100mph, and

My old gas boat, *Rhonda*, built by Riley Beasley in 1947. *Left to right*: Herbert Lange and Travis Morris. Wilson Snowden took the picture from a 23-foot skiff built in 1948 that I carried my float box and decoys in. I still have this skiff in 2014. *Author's collection.*

it broke it that night. Frances said never again would the two most important men in her life be in that sound at night at the same time. I know she was worried to death, but I had no way to communicate with her.

The next morning, the Coast Guard helicopter found Mr. Charles safe at Swan Island. His motor had broken down, and he had poled through the marsh to Swan Island. They picked him up. Us and the Coast Guard boys headed back to Jones' Dock at Waterlily. They were running in the lee of us, and sometimes their boat was standing up so straight I thought it was going to blow over backward. Three times *Rhonda* stuck her bow so far down that seas broke on the front of the cabin. The helicopter said it was blowing 72mph when we were coming back.

After I finished developing Corolla Village and Monkey Island was sold, I really didn't use the boat that much. It was just a trip to Waterlily every day to make sure the pump was working.

I don't remember what year it was, but we were having a real cold winter, and we were having a problem with the blower motor on the furnace in our house. I was in Elizabeth City at Aubrey Snowden's place, Quick Electric, when I got a call from Jimmy Jones saying my boat was sunk. I told him where I was and that I'd be there as soon as I could. I called Jimmy Markert, the caretaker at Piney Island Club, and asked him to take our big pump and get "Hambone" to help him and see if he could get her pumped up.

When I got there, she was pumped up. Mr. Frank Carter was at the dock and heard me say, "If I can give her to somebody she will belong to somebody before the sun sets tonight." Mr. Frank said his son, Walton Carter, would take it.

The weather was freezing, and the problem turned out to be that water had frozen in one of the exhaust pipes and busted it.

Walton Carter pulled it up, took the engine out of it and gave it to somebody. Levie Bunch Jr. got the steering wheel and some of the hardware. The boat ended up back here in my shelter until my son, Walton, needed to put a piece of equipment in the shelter, and he got Julian Bray to tear it up and take it to the dump.

This has been a lot about my old boat *Rhonda*, but she deserved it. That boat made me more money and gave me more pleasure than any one piece of equipment I have ever owned. I carried people to the Currituck Outer Banks and sold them land when there was no road over there, and it carried me, my friends and sportsmen duck hunting many, many times. When I sent it to the dump, I'd given up on getting any of these old boats restored. Now that we are able to get some of them restored, I wish I hadn't sent it to the dump.

From 1970 until 1979 was probably the happiest time of my life. I love Currituck Sound, and during that time I had a legitimate excuse to be on it nearly every day, either taking people to the beach to see land or duck hunting. I was doing what I wanted to do and making a decent living for my family.

BOB MORSE

Bob Morse lived on Church's Island (Waterlily) and is famous for the duck decoys he made. You don't hear much about the boats he built. I'll tell you about the ones I know of.

He built a big cabin boat for Monkey Island Club to take people and supplies back and forth to the island. When I was working at Mr. Pat O'Neal's boat shop, Mr. George Twiford, who was the Monkey Island caretaker then, brought it to the shop to have it repaired. After pulling it up, Mr. Pat said it wasn't worth fixing. He got me to strip all the hardware from it, and we burnt the boat up. He gave me the porthole out of the front of the cabin, and I put it in *Rhonda*.

The Monkey Island boat built by Bob Morse. It is on Grissie Barco's railway. *Faye Barco Hooper.*

This boat is similar to the one Bob Morse built for Mr. Dexter Snow. *Grace Austin.*

Bob Morse built a little kinda' speedboat for Mr. Dexter Snow. It was about 20 feet long and decked all the way over where the engine was to make two cockpits. It had a flathead V8 Ford motor, and the boat was flat bottom. This was when they were racing gas boats in Dowdy's Bay.

When I was just a young boy, Mr. Ray Adams, who owned the Whalehead Club, sent Jarvis Snow to Poplar Branch in this boat to pick me up to hunt with Mr. Adams one day when my daddy couldn't go. Jarvis' daddy, Dexter Snow, was superintendent of the Whalehead Club for Mr. Adams. Jarvis told me this boat ended up being sold to somebody in Florida.

The only other boat I remember Bob Morse building was a flat bottom boat about 25 feet long. It had a rather long cabin and a shelter cabin top that went all the way to the stern. I don't know who he built it for or what happened to it, but the boat stayed tied to a stake in front of Mr. Morse's house when I remember it. While I'm thinking about it, Grissie Barco helped Bob Morse build boats.

Jimmy Hayman's boat at Jones' Dock in Waterlily. *Author's collection.*

When Teat Collins was carrying the mail from Waterlily to Corolla, he had a pretty little deadrise boat about 23 feet long with a cabin and windshield. It had a flathead V8 Ford motor with a car transmission. It would run faster in second gear than it would in high. I'm sure this was because of the size of the propeller. The last time I saw the boat, it was tied up in a creek by a little bridge before you get to the old S-curved bridge in Hertford.

Jimmy Hayman had a flat bottom gas boat about 23 feet long with a box tunnel and six-cylinder Ford motor hooked up straight. It had a cabin with a windshield and would run along right good. It was planked fore and aft but was flat bottom. The boat was in Hayman's mill yard until Jimmy died, then Jo Ann let the man that had the antique shop in Jarvisburg with all the old boats and things in the yard have the boat. The last time I saw the boat, it was growing up in vines in the back of his yard. I'm not sure who made the boat, but I think it was made in Grandy by an Evans or Dowdy.

Mr. Frank Carter had a 32-foot shad boat that was built in 1906 by Otis Dough in Wanchese. It was named *Red Wing* when Dexter Snow had it because it had a Red Wing motor. During prohibition, Dexter Snow used this boat to haul liquor from East Lake to Gallop's Landing in Powell's Point. Mr. Dexter's brother, Marchant, had a boat just like it hauling the same thing. It caught fire in Albemarle Sound, and he and Abraham Gallop both lost their lives.

After Mr. Dexter had the *Red Wing*, it ended up around Great Bridge, Virginia. Mr. Frank Carter got it from there in the 1960s.

Above: The *Gray Goose* at the Wright Brothers landing at Deep Creek in Jarvisburg. *Author's collection.*

Left: The boat Albert Sumrell built for Ray Adams, owner of the Whalehead Club, to take people and supplies to and from the Whalehead Club. *Author's collection.*

Walton Carter, Frank Carter's son, rebuilt that boat in 1978 and had Bruce Bess fiberglass it. He changed the name to the *Gray Goose*, and it's a good thing the boat can't talk. That's all I'm going to say about that.

When Walton Carter quit using his float box hunting, he sold the boat to Jerry Wright, who was going to preserve it for the Whalehead Trust. It was blocked up at his landing in Jarvisburg when Hurricane Irene came through with the real high tide and floated it out in the marsh. Jerry Wright told me he got it out of the marsh in the fall of 2013 and now has it in his boat house at Deep Creek in Jarvisburg.

Albert Sumrell

After Mr. Ray Adams bought the Whalehead Club in 1940, he needed another gas boat besides the shad boat he had to take people and supplies from Poplar Branch Landing to the Whalehead Club.

Mr. Adams got my daddy, Chester Morris (who was his attorney), to check with Mr. Pat O'Neal to see how much he would charge to build him a gas boat. Best I remember it was $100 per foot plus the engine, cabin and so on. Mr. Adams wouldn't pay that.

Mr. Adams had bought the old Penny Hill Coast Guard station from the government and had it moved to the grounds of the Whalehead Club. He got Mr. Albert Sumrell to build him a gas boat, and he built it in the boathouse part of the Penny Hill Station. The boat was probably 28 feet and flat bottomed. It had a cabin and shelter cabin and was pretty wide. Jarvis Snow told me that at one time she was leaking so bad if she was at Poplar Branch Landing he'd have to get up in the middle of the night and go pump her out to keep her from sinking. Again, this was before automatic bilge pumps.

After Mr. Adams died and the Whalehead Club was sold, the boat changed hands several times. Henry Hampton was the last one who had it as a gas boat. "Hambone" bought it from him and knocked the cabin and skeg off it, and he and I used it to haul lumber to Corolla to build Kenyon Wilson's and the Copelands' houses on the oceanfront in Corolla. Then I bought it from "Hambone" to use for building blinds at Monkey Island. When I finished with it, I gave it to Donnie Jones to use for a bulkhead in front of his house.

Point Harbor: Allen Hayman

Mr. Hayman was Bobby Sullivan's granddaddy. Bobby is known for the sport fisherman boats he has built.

Back in the 1950s, when they were racing boats in Dowdy's Bay, Mr. Charlie Wright (Dr. Wright's daddy) got Mr. Allen Hayman to build him a boat. It was about 22 feet long. It had a step in the bottom like the *Phyllis Rae* that Mr. Pat O'Neal built for Mr. Orville Woodhouse.

The boat was open with no cabin or spray hood at the time. It had a six-cylinder Chevrolet hooked up straight. Mr. Charlie carried me perch fishing in that boat one time.

After Mr. Charlie died, Bill Riddick got his hunting rig, including this boat. When I was helping Bill Riddick guide with this boat, the step had been taken out and I think lengthened and a cabin put on it that was open in the back.

When Bill Riddick built a new boat, I think it was pulled up and put in the woods at John Jr. Wright's landing on Deep Creek behind the Cotton Gin.

Mr. Ray Adams had a pretty dory that Mr. Allen Hayman built for him in the 1940s. When Mr. Adams had beach parties at the Whalehead Club in the summertime, some of the men that worked there that knew what they were doing would take this dory, set a net and catch fish for a fish fry.

In the 1970s, Griggs O'Neal had the dory because I tried to buy it from him and he wouldn't sell it. The last time I saw the dory, it was in front of Barry Nelms' Walnut Island Restaurant in Grandy with flowers in it.

I remember an old 32- or 33-foot battery boat that G.C. Sawyer had at Hog Quarter Landing. It was probably the same one his daddy had.

Wilton Walker

Mr. Wilton should have been at the first of this section because he was at Tull's Creek. I started at Coinjock with the boat builders and went south. Mr. Wilton lived on Tull's Creek road, and his shop was at the Launch on Tull's Bay, which is about twelve miles north of Coinjock. I'm going to include some pictures of some of the boats Mr. Wilton built. I don't remember those boats because I wasn't around his shop as much as I was Mr. Pat O'Neal's.

Boating and Fishing in Old Currituck

Mr. Wilton Walker at the Launch, standing in the water by a boat he had built. *Glenna Walker Alcock.*

Mr. Wilton Walker built this boat. I think he built it for Dr. Lee, who retired at Point Harbor. *Glenna Walker Alcock.*

I'll tell you what I do remember seeing at Mr. Wilton's shop. I was up there one day when he and Big John were putting a 671 Detroit in a big boat he was building. He had the engine on two big poles from the ground up to the washboards. He had a line tied around the engine and tied to an A John Deere tractor on the other side of the boat. He pulled it up to the washboards with the tractor. Then he had a chainfall up in the top of his shop centered over where he wanted to lower the engine. He hooked that to the engine and picked it up, then lowered it down in the boat.

63

Boat built by Wilton Walker. *Glenna Walker Alcock.*

Boat built by Wilton Walker. *Glenna Walker Alcock.*

Another thing I saw Mr. Wilton do when he was building one of those big boats was how he got the shear line. He ran a string from the bow to the stern that had a lot of metal washers on it. He kept moving the washers until he got the shear like he wanted it, then he cut the ribs off there.

Mr. Wilton built a sailboat for Carter Lindsey, Mr. Frank Brumsey's nephew. Carter eventually weighed six hundred pounds. Carter, Joe Jr. Ferrell and W.L. Northern were all several years older than me, but sometimes they'd let me tag along with them on the sailboat.

Mr. Wilton Walker built this sail boat for Carter Lindsey. Joe Jr. Ferrell is standing on the boat. Carter is in the water. I sailed on the boat some when I was a kid. Carter and the other boys that hung around with him were older than me, but sometimes they'd let me tag along. Daddy gave Carter five dollars to teach me how to swim. *Mary Ellen Snowden Williams.*

Mr. Wilton built another sailboat just like Carter's for Yates Barbara. I don't know where either of the boats ended up.

NEWTON HAMPTON

Newton Hampton is seventy-six years old and still building skiffs as of this writing in 2014. Newton's family's farm joins my family's farm in Coinjock, although the Postal Service calls it Barco now.

Newton farmed his family's farm until his son, Lindsey, got old enough for him to turn it over to him. Somewhere down the line, Newton got a contract to deliver the mail from Coinjock to Point Harbor. As the population increased, so did the mail carriers. Now he only has one route and hires somebody to do that. He has always helped his son with the farming in his spare time.

In *Currituck Sports*. *Left to right*: Newton Hampton, Ed O'Neal, Ralph Berry, Graham Keaton and Ronnie Phelps. Travis Morris took the picture. *Author's collection.*

This picture is not about boats, but is about Newton, and I think worth telling about. Newton lives right across the road from Currituck Sports. Every morning at about 5:30 a.m. or 6:00 a.m., Newton fixes a mug of coffee for him and Ed O'Neal, who owns Currituck Sports. Ed opens at 5:00 a.m. Next, Gerald Gray, who drives the mail truck, stops by on his way to Elizabeth City to pick up the mail and brings the news from down Powell's Point way. Then Judy Berry brings Ralph "Butch" and drops him off. Ronnie Phelps comes about that time from Waterlily. He doesn't come everyday, but if he does he keeps us entertained, especially telling stories about how tight his neighbor and fishing partner, Mr. Bishop, is. He also does a lot of fishing with cane poles and keeps us in fish. At 6:30 a.m., Graham Keaton and I come. We all solve the world's problems, but it doesn't seem to help any. At exactly 7:15 a.m., Graham gets up and has to go see if Miss Carol has breakfast ready, unless he is playing golf; then he leaves about 7:00 a.m. At 7:20 a.m., Newton says it's time for him to go across the road and get a bowl of cereal. Jo Ann and I eat at 6:00 a.m., so I've already had my breakfast. I take "Butch" home, and Ronnie gets his minnows if he is going fishing; if not, he leaves when we do.

This is just a little example of what goes on around country stores. I'm sure there are several other gathering places like that in the county—in fact, I'm sure all over the country.

It reminds me of when Jack Helms ran a store (it's now B.J.'s Restaurant). All the people I'm talking about in the next couple of paragraphs are dead, including Jack, John Jr. and Snookie Wright; Charlie and Lawrence

Jr. Dozier; G.C. Sawyer; Roy Sawyer; and I don't know who else. John Jr. and Charlie were good friends in the summertime, but come duck hunting season, they were dire enemies. Charlie would do anything he could that he knew would aggravate John Jr. in hunting season. John Jr. fed the geese at the end of the dock at Dew's Island. I hauled potatoes for both the Wrights and the Doziers. I got along with all of them. Charlie had this little speedboat, and one day during hunting season I was riding with him. He was running her as fast as she would go and ran right up to the dock at Dew's Island and spun her around, almost hitting the dock, running the geese away. I put my face down. I didn't want John Jr. to even see me in the boat.

John Jr. built a little arch bridge across Deep Creek from the mainland to Dew's Island. Charlie told me he put a windshield on his gas boat just so it wouldn't get under the bridge and made John Jr. put a draw in the bridge because it is navigable waters. You raised it with a block and tackle. This is just such things as they did, and I'm sure John Jr. did just as much to aggravate Charlie. Now back to what this book is supposed to be about.

Newton is not a boat builder by trade. He is a farmer, but he is a person of many talents. The first boat he built, Oscar Roberts helped him build. It was 16.5 feet long and wide for the length. He first had an outboard motor on it. This boat was built out of plywood. He later got Mr. Pat O'Neal to help him put a tunnel and an inboard six-cylinder Pontiac motor in the boat. Newton sold the boat to Brownie Melson, who sold it to Mark Doxey, and I don't know what happened to it from there. He built this boat around 1960.

Next he built a little deadrise skiff that he still owns. He just rebuilt that skiff last year. That makes that skiff fifty-four years old.

After that, he got hooked up with Raynor Collins, building row skiffs for the City of Lexington, North Carolina. He built ten, and then Raynor got a contract for him to build ten more. He was building on those skiffs when his daddy died in March of 1963. At the time, he was living in a house on Coinjock Development Road next to Harrison's Marina. He had built him a little shop behind his house. He had built five of the second ten when his daddy died. He got Raynor to finish the other five. He already had a lot of the lumber cut out. All he had to do was put them together. After his daddy died, he had to go to full-time farming.

Clyde Scaff had helped Newton build his shop. Clyde furnished everything for the boat, and Newton built him a plywood runabout. Sometime along about that time Newton and Graham Keaten both built plywood runabouts that they were racing.

A skiff Newton Hampton is framing up. *Newton Hampton.*

In 1981, Newton built a skiff for his cousin Barry Walker. Barry still uses the skiff to take sportsmen duck hunting in. Next he built a skiff for Mike Merrell. He built that all out of plywood. In between all this, Mr. Pat O'Neal built Newton a gas boat with a concave tunnel. Newton helped him, but it was Mr. Pat's know-how that built it. This boat was later sold to Mr. Earl Slick for Narrows Island. When they went to outboards, it was sold several times, and I don't know where it ended up.

Next, Newton built a boat for Lee Riggs in Elizabeth City. Then he built one for Beetle-Bum Doxey. That was an 18-foot skiff.

The last one he built was for Mark Conwell. This one had a regular juniper bottom. He didn't want any plywood in it.

A skiff Newton Hampton completed; taken in front of his shop in Barco. *Newton Hampton.*

    Somewhere back along the way he built a 21-foot skiff to carry his float box on. He still has this skiff, with the float box still on it like he last used it, which was probably thirty years ago.

    Newton also repaired three skiffs for Wilson Snowden. I think two of them were for the Whalehead Preservation Trust and are in the boathouse in Corolla now.

Carl Ross

Now I'm going to tell you about the youngest man I know of in Currituck that still builds skiffs. Carl is sixty-one years old as of 2014. He started building boats in his spare time after the hunting season in 1983 when he was superintendent of Currituck Shooting Club.

Tillman Merrell was building a skiff, and Carl went over there to watch him to see how he was setting it up. Tillman had built boats before for himself and his brother, Elmer, but the bottom and the stem post on those boats were straighter and they had low, straight sides like a Van Caroon boat.

Tillman had been over to look at James Guard's boat, which was a Milford Austin boat. The boat Tillman was building looked more like that.

Carl built his first boat like that, then he built a little square-ended boat for poling around in the ponds at Currituck Club. He got the pattern for that from Winton Outlaw. Winton worked at Pine Island Club and had built a little square-ended bateau out of plywood to pole around the marsh to feed the ducks. Carl built his out of juniper. Then he made Andy Newbern one, made his brother one and made the club one.

Carl said he didn't have the equipment he needed to build boats. He was having to go to Elizabeth City Shipyard and get Mary Hadley Griffin, who owned the shipyard, to get his lumber planed, or sometimes he could get Mr. Hoskins down the county to plane it. He said he had to learn how to pick his lumber out and where to get it and all that. He got most of his lumber from Bill Beatty in Manteo. He also got lumber from Jones Lumber Company and Gates Milling, and he bought some in Columbia. Moses White was already out of business by the time Carl was building boats. Moses White was where I always got juniper to repair my old gas boats. He first had a shingle mill on the road through the dismal swamp, but later he had a little lumberyard on 158 before you get to the swamp that he sold juniper from.

Around 1985, Milford Austin decided he was going to get out of building boats, so Carl went over there and bought his planer. It was a 1978 planer. It was a nice heavy-duty Rockwell. He gave him a price and said he'd throw in the stretchers. He said he'd never build another boat again. He had stretchers for 15-, 16- and 18-foot boats. They hold the boat apart when you are framing it; two to the boat.

Carl went and talked to Billy Corbell, and Billy said, "Here's how you do it [talking about the bottom]. If your setup boards are 18 feet long

Boating and Fishing in Old Currituck

Milford Austin and Carl Ross in Carl's shop. *Author's collection.*

A skiff Carl Ross was building. *Carl Ross.*

and you have to match them, you are going to marry them together so they are twins. Come back one third from the bow once you cut your bow streak in. If it's a six-twelve or four-twelve, however, you want it to come back one third, then take about two and a quarter to two and a half inches out. If you take anymore than that, it's going to be too straight."

Carl said instead of using a pattern each time, he figured it out like that, and it worked. Here is something else Billy told Carl: "The whole thing is about the displacing of water. Joe Hayman wanted to tuck 'em in. You don't need to do that. You are not a sailboat anymore, and you are not just a putt-putt boat. Just let it come back and then you've got more lift."

Carl said that Billy Corbell built some model boats that are really nice. They are to scale. I remember when he built a little gas boat for himself. It was a pretty little boat. I don't know what ever became of it. At one time Billy built the cabins on the gas boats that Mr. Pat O'Neal built.

By 1987 Carl had a shop built, and he started building boats. He'd build four a year. Milford Austin was retired from the Coast Guard Base in Elizabeth City. He was a sheet metal worker. It wasn't long before he was coming over to Carl's shop. Dailey Williams would go down to his shop, kinda' like some of us go to the Bait Shop here mornings.

Milford would go to Hardee's in Grandy first, then he'd go up to Carl's to see what he was doing. So Carl told him if he was going to go up there everyday to let him hire him. Carl told Milford he could show Carl the tricks of the trade. They started building boats, and people knew Milford was up there and they started putting some boats out. They'd do four a year. It would get too hot in the summertime, then it would soon be time to start fixing blinds for duck season.

Carl said Jimmy K. Wyatt has the first boat he ever built. Walton Carter has three skiffs Carl built. He built Bootie Spruill a net skiff 22 feet long.

Carl told me he'd built somewhere between fifty and sixty boats.

Shoving Poles

We need to talk just a little bit about shoving poles. That is an essential piece of equipment in Currituck Sound. The first shoving poles I had when I was young I got from Mr. George Brice up on Maple Road. He had a blacksmith shop and made ash shoving poles as well as other things, like duck heads sawed out on a band saw (you had to finish carving them with a pocket knife and sandpaper).

I used to get shoving poles from Joe Hayman. I'd get twelve footers to keep in the little skiffs and gas boat. I had two sixteen footers I kept in my float box skiff. There is still one Joe Hayman sixteen footer in my son Walton's warehouse now. Then I've had some Dailey Williams poles. Daily made a really good pole. He put some time in them. I still have two sixteen footers little Wallace O'Neal made.

I've had poles that Billy Beasley made. They were crude, but Billy could make a good pole because he made my wife Jo Ann one that is just as nice a pole as you could ever ask for, but that's the only one I've ever seen that he made like that.

Carl said Tillman Merrell made some shoving poles. He made them kinda' square on the end so they wouldn't roll around.

Newton Hampton still makes shoving poles, and he makes a good pole. Ed sells them over at Currituck Sports.

Shoving poles need to be made out of ash. Sometimes Newton has to go a long ways to get the ash. I bought one of his poles last year and hung it up in my shop just so I'd have it. I'll probably never use it, but I'm sure one of my grandsons will come after it one day.

Other Boats

Here are pictures of some other well-known boats that were in Currituck that were not all built here.

Ambrose "Hambone" Twiford running the 32-foot Monkey Island shad boat built in 1916 by Otis Dough of Wanchese. Levie Bunch was the last owner of this boat. He donated it to the Whalehead Preservation Trust, who had it restored. It is now in the boathouse across the road from the Currituck Beach Lighthouse.

Ambrose "Hambone" Twiford running the 32-foot Monkey Island shad boat built by Otis Dough of Wanchese in 1916. *Author's collection.*

Lemara. This boat had two open cockpits. Mr. Joseph P. Knapp had it sent to Mackey Island from New York in 1925. Mr. Knapp was a very wealthy man from New York who came to Currituck duck hunting. He liked it here, bought Mackey Island and built his home there. He was a great benefactor to Currituck County. In 1932, he gave the county more money than the citizens paid in county taxes, mostly to the schools. He founded More Game Birds in America, which is the predecessor to Ducks Unlimited.

The *Lemara. North Carolina Wildlife Museum in Corolla.*

The *Bootlegger*. This was another boat Mr. Knapp had sent to Currituck. I don't know where either this boat or the *Lemara* was built. I remember this boat coming to Currituck Wharf to pick up Mr. Knapp. My daddy, Chester Morris, was an attorney that represented Mr. Knapp, and I can remember him sending the *Bootlegger* to pick up Daddy. If roses were in bloom, Mrs. Knapp would always send Mama some by Daddy.

The Currituck Post Office was right in the curve across from the wharf. When I was a little boy, we lived at Currituck, and I hung out a lot with Mr. Hall, the postmaster. Mr. Knapp would wait for the *Bootlegger* to pick him up in the post office, where it was warm. I remember when Mr. Hall introduced me to Mr. Knapp. What I remember most was that he was a big man with a big overcoat, and I was a little boy.

The *Bootlegger* at Mr. Knapp's home on Mackey Island. *North Carolina Wildlife Museum in Corolla.*

The last time I remember seeing the *Bootlegger*, it was tied up by the bridge in Moyock Creek. Mr. Dudley Bagley was friends with Mr. Knapp, and he got the boat after Mr. Knapp died. I don't know what happened to the boat after that.

One more thing I remember about the boat was it had a Buda engine in it.

The *Cygnett*. This was a boat built in Connecticut that was owned by the Currituck Shooting Club. They used it to bring the members from the train at Munden's Point in the north end of the sound to Currituck Club.

The *Cygnett*. *Carl Ross.*

Croatan. This boat was built for Mr. Russell Griggs, who, with his wife, Miss Bernie, owned the Croatan Hotel in Kill Devil Hills and Hampton Lodge in Waterlily. I owned the boat when this picture was taken in 1975. *Left to right*: "Hambone," Herbert Lange, Shirley Austin and Travis Morris. We caught these big bluefish in the surf at Corolla. Shirley had changed her clothes to go somewhere on the mainland.

The *Croatan*. *Left to right*: "Hambone," Herbert Lange, Shirley Austin and Travis Morris. *Author's collection.*

Whalehead Club shad boat. *Author's collection.*

This shad boat came with the Whalehead property when Mr. Adams bought it in 1940. The house in the background is the superintendent's house, which burned in the late 1960s. I have been on this boat when she was loaded to the gills with groceries, baggage and guests on their way from Poplar Branch to the Whalehead Club.

Casey Jones' dock in Waterlily. The white gas boat belonged to Ambrose "Hambone" Twiford at the time. It had belonged to Casey Jones. I think he got the boat from a hunting club in Back Bay, Virginia. I remember when he got the boat. It had to have a lot of work done to it. He brought it to Grissie Barco's railway, and they pulled it up and worked on it for a long time. (Grissie had a railway where he repaired a lot of boats. He also built skiffs.) At the time, the boat had a shelter cabin on it. The motor was a 283 Chevrolet with Bar water-cooled manifolds and a marine transmission. The boat was originally built in 1906 by Otis Dough in Wanchese. Levie Bunch ended up with the boat and gave it to the Whalehead Preservation Trust, who had it restored by Bobby Sullivan, and the boat is now in the dry boathouse in Corolla. Casey sold the boat to "Hambone," who later traded it to Levie Bunch for a fiberglass motor lifeboat.

Ambrose "Hambone" Twiford's fishing rig at Jones' Dock in Waterlily. The boat in the right corner of the picture is Elijah Tate's gas boat. Note the galvanized hand pump standing up by the corner of the cabin. *Author's collection.*

The last trip from Monkey Island before the sound froze over. The *Corolla Express* was the only boat I had with fiberglass that I could run in the ice. There was ice in the sound on this trip. The deck on the stern of the boat was slicked over with ice. My raincoat was a solid sheet of ice. I think this was around 1976. I had to get the Coast Guard helicopter to take the caretaker, Jack Jarvis, and his wife, Sylvia, and her mother off the island a few days later. The sound froze over so hard that Buddy Ponton walked to Monkey Island. He pulled along a little johnboat in case he broke through the ice.

I don't remember the name of the first man on the left on the dock, but the next man is Sid Tayloe, who was CEO of Yadkin Valley Bank in

The *Corolla Express*. Mr. Pat O'Neal built this boat for Bill Riddick in 1954. Years later, Bill Riddick got Mr. Charlie Wright's hunting rig, and he had this boat upside down under a tree in his yard for ten years. Travis Morris bought the boat in 1973. Wilson Snowden helped him fix it up and fiberglass it. This picture shows the last trip from Monkey Island before the sound froze over around 1976. *Author's collection.*

Elkin, North Carolina. Next to him are Dr. Doyle Pruitt and Dr. Eldon Parks. They were all from Elkin. I later sold them and some more men from Elkin 125 acres of marsh in Corolla with enough high land next to Lighthouse Pond to build a clubhouse and a helicopter pad for Floyd Brendell's helicopter. He was a member of the club. They built a big clubhouse. I think it had eight bedrooms and a big cupola on top with a fireplace so they could look out all over the marsh. They named it Lighthouse Club. Don't get this confused with the first Lighthouse Club, which is what Mr. Edward Collins Knight bought and built on what he called Corolla Island. When Mr. Adams bought it, he named it the Whalehead Club. This was 4.5 miles sound to ocean. So much for that history lesson.

I took this picture from the bridge at the Whalehead Club in 1947 of "Buggins" (Saint Clair) Lewark's boat. People called him "Buggins" because he was always bugging folks about something. He was putting in bulkhead for Mr. Adams and living on the boat. He was also a federal game warden.

"Buggins" (Saint Clair) Lewark's boat in 1947. *Author's collection.*

Hand-Crafted Boats of Old Currituck

Grissie Barco's round-stern gas boat at Waterlily. *Faye Barco Hooper.*

This shows boats and their owners' names at Jones' Dock in Waterlily. *Author's collection.*

I'm going to list the people in Currituck that I know of who built boats in Currituck, though I'm sure it's by no means all the people that built boats. Most all these people had other jobs. Building boats was a sideline. I'm going to start at Tull's Creek and go south:

Wilton Walker	Carl Ross
John Fisk	Johnny Guard
Billy Corbell	Milford Austin
Newton Hampton	Wilson Corbell
Pat O'Neal	Carl Beasley
Billy Beasley	Richard Dowdy
Joe Hayman	F.A. Dowdy
Raynor Collins	Floyd Parker
Riley Beasley	Seth Garrington
Grissie Barco	Allen Hayman
Bob Morse	Bobby Sullivan
Worth Morse	Burvell Beasley
Blanton Saunders	

PART II
COMMERCIAL FISHING ON THE OUTER BANKS

What we are going to talk about now is history because between the new regulations and the tourist industry, commercial fishing on the Currituck Outer Banks is just about a thing of the past.

In my last book, *Stories of Old Currituck Outer Banks*, I told a little about Mr. and Mrs. Thomas Ponton moving to Corolla with their two sons, Buddy and Andy, in 1967. Since that time, their son Buddy has become a legend when it comes to commercial fishing on the Currituck Outer Banks. I would also like to say that although they are not native Outer Bankers, the Ponton family has been accepted as prominent residents of Corolla Village.

I have known and been friends with Buddy since 1970. I have seen him go to sea with his crew in a dory many times when it was way too rough to go to sea in a dory, but the fish were running and Buddy was going to sea. The signature of his dories was a red shark's mouth, wide open, with white teeth painted on each side of the bow.

Buddy Ponton, Thomas Ponton and Andy Ponton mending a net. *Annie Ponton.*

Top: Mrs. Thomas Ponton (Antha) in her foul weather gear. *Annie Ponton.*

Left: Annie Ponton, Buddy's wife, standing by two dories that Buddy built with his signature shark's mouth painted on the bow of each. *Annie Ponton.*

Last Saturday afternoon, I spent an hour and a half with a tape recorder talking to Buddy in his home. He doesn't fish in the ocean commercially anymore. He has a few restaurants that he supplies fish and crabs for that he catches in Currituck Sound. His wife, Annie, is the housekeeping supervisor for Twiddy & Company Realtors in Corolla.

I'm going to let Buddy Ponton tell you in his own words (with some editing by RM) what it's like to go to sea through the surf in a dory full of net and coming back, hopefully, with a boatload of fish. Fish or not, coming back through that surf is just as dangerous, if not more dangerous, than going out.

Buddy Ponton's Story

I started fishing up behind Penny's Hill. I had a camp up there right after I got out of high school in 1961. I married Ellen, my first wife, while I was up in Virginia, and I had bought some property in Virginia while I was working up there, plus I'd bought this property down here. This is the old Cleveland and Tillman Lewark tract. Norris Austin had the deal, and at the time he didn't have enough money to pull the whole deal off, so he asked me if I wanted to get in on it. Norris wanted the half that had the house on it. That's what helped me get down here. We put the camp I had at Penny's Hill on wheels and moved it right down here. While we were building these two houses [his daddy's and his], *we stayed in the camp.*

If it was really rough when we were fishing, all the people in the village thought we weren't going to get back to the beach, particularly in the wintertime when we were fishing gill nets about two miles off shore. They'd go over to the beach and sit there on the beach to see if we could get back in. We could tell about how rough the surf was by how many cars were sitting out there on the beach to see us come back in. We've sunk 'em before, but most of the time we got back in. If we sunk 'em, we'd sink 'em right in the wash. I always told the boys, "As soon as you think you can touch bottom, jump out because a dory, the way they are built, will roll up on their side, and you don't want to dump all your fish out after working all morning (or sometimes all day)." What we'd do, the boys would jump out on both sides and we'd slide it in. It might be sunk, but then we'd hook a truck to it and then kinda' ease it up out of the water while the boys would be bailing with five-gallon buckets, plus a lot of water would run out the well because we had the motor inside the boat.

I asked Griggs one time [Griggs O'Neal was deputy sheriff in Corolla], *"What's everybody coming over here for when we are coming in; does everybody want a mess of fish, because we give fish to everybody?" He said, "Oh no, we thought it was too rough and we didn't think you were gonna' make it back in." I said, "Oh, we're coming back, Griggs."*

Along that same line, one day when Cuz was down at Nunnemaker's [seafood packing company], *it had been rough all week, and we were the only ones fishing. We were fishing haul seine. It had been right touch and go. We hadn't sunk any that week, and we were making big hauls, like ten thousand pounds or better with nearly every haul. Charles Nunnemaker told Cuz, he said, "It's kinda' tight up there, boys. Y'all still going?" Cuz said, "Well, you know Buddy; as long as he's catching fish, he's going to sea." And*

Charles said, "Yeah, you always got to go, but you don't always have to come back." [They told us that in Coast Guard Boot Camp.—TM] *I had a good crew, and they were good, able-bodied boys. Everybody was young. That makes a lot of difference. I'd hate to be doing that stuff now.*

One day, we turned over setting the haul seine right here in front of the lighthouse. The motor came out. We lost the motor. We were hitting about the third sandbar out. It was really rough. We just stood her right up, and she came over backward. We were about 150 yards out, and we had to swim ashore. The dory was kinda' to the end of the haul seine, so the guys on the end at the beach just start pulling net, pulling it backward. They were just trying to get us in.

The thing about sinking in the ocean when you are around the bar is this: it's in close to shore, and you can't stay tied to the boat. Everybody always says stay with the boat. Ain't no such thing as staying around a boat when the seas are hitting you and knocking you around really bad. That day we swam on ashore fine. We got everything ashore but the motor. I wanted to get that motor back, so me and Andy, my brother, went the next day. We set this gill net. Well we didn't never get it all set, and we turned that one over end over end. We were coming back in that time. We had already set around where the motor was and were coming in and got too big a sea behind us, and I couldn't outrun it, and it just kept picking us up and picking us up. It was a 26-foot boat. It picked us up so the bow actually drove down into the water, and the last time I saw Andy and the rest of that gill net, it was throwing him out of the boat because he was way up over top of me then. It was just like you had a sling shot. All that net and him went overboard. We were out probably a couple hundred yards. When Andy came up, all I could see was all this monofilament net all over the top of him. I could just see his head sticking up. I started swimming toward him because he was fouled in the gear. He went down, and then the next time he came up, he was clear of everything. We swam on ashore. The guys were already pulling the net and everything. It got hung up on something. The boat wouldn't come. It just stayed out there. It was a big out suck there, and it wouldn't come through that suck. Every time it got close to coming across that bar, it would suck it back out just like they call a riptide now that swimmers get in.

When my brother was in high school, he was on the all-city swim league in Norfolk. He was really good at swimming—far better than I was. We tied a half-inch line around his waist and he swam out there, and we got as far as we could get, like chest deep, feeding him line (and this was in March, so there wasn't anything warm about it). He swam out there and tied it on to the dory ring on the bow so we could pull that boat in.

T.M: Did y'all have foul weather gear on?

We had foul weather gear when it turned over.

T.M: How do you swim with that stuff on?

You can. You know they always tell you that you want to kick your boots off and everything when you are overboard. I sunk one time when we were fishing up at the Virginia line. It was in January and I had just bought my hip boots I had on, and I was curling my toes trying to keep from losing those boots, because when you swim they will come on off. I lost one boot, and years later, a guy told me that was fishing with Jimmy Austin out of Nags Head. He said, "You know, we were going down the beach one day when y'all sunk up there, and I found a boot on the beach. I always meant to give you that boot, and I never did see you for two or three years. I thought I'd tell you." I said, "Damn, man, that boot was brand new!"

The first time I ever did sink in the ocean, I did try to get out of the boots, but with the oil skins and everything, if it's real cold, I think the more layers you got on it takes it a little while for the water to get to you. When it's really cold when you sink and that water hits your chest, it's just like trying to blow all that air right out of you, or it was with me. It's not so bad when it gets around your waist, but when it comes on up your chest, you know it.

We didn't sink all the time, but over the years we probably sank five, six or seven times, and usually it was pretty rough when we did it. If it was really cold weather, the guys on the beach would take one truck and they'd cut the heater wide open, and then when you got ashore you just stripped down all the way and jumped in the truck. If you left anything on then put clothes on over top of them they get wet, and it's still cold outside.

I remember me and Pete Nixon sank up there by the Virginia line rock fishing. That was the coldest I think I've ever been in my life when we went overboard. I think the fish were there, but we never got them that day.

Another time I can think of was kind of a weird situation. I reckon it's almost opposite to the way things are today. Everybody worries about these dolphin and everything. It was late fall or early winter, and we had the rock net in the boat. It had a long wing on it; there was probably three quarters of mile of net in the boat. The wing end of it was eight-inch net.

There was a bunch of dolphin coming down the beach from the north. All the water in front of 'em was really muddy, otherwise the water was fairly clear, so we figured they were pushing a school of fish; we just didn't have a clue what kind it was. We couldn't see anything breaking. We went on down ahead of them about a half mile, and we set out and just had it outside. We dropped the wing outside and come on ashore with the warp line, just like we would set for spot, roundhead or anything like that.

We've done this before, and when these dolphin get to that warp line coming ashore, they turn and go on around the net. If there was anything hung in the net, they might pick at the net. They'd bite the heads or tails or whatever was sticking out of the net, but this time they went on down in the net, so we started hauling, figuring they were feeding on something. Generally speaking, if we ever had any dolphins in the net, they'd just stick their heads on the top and go on out.

This day, we get the wing in and we got a dolphin right there in the end. There was another rig there from Colington. Those boys that were fishing on that rig and the guys I could turn loose on my rig all got overboard, and they freed the dolphin and sent him on his way. It ended up we caught about twenty dolphin that day fouled in the webbing. It was all nylon net. The guys released 'em all, but five of 'em washed back up on shore, dead. There were no roads or anything out there at the time. The only vehicle we could see at the time was the guy that used to set traps for the gypsy moths for the state.

Arnold Daniels and Billy Biggs called me that night around eleven o'clock. This moth trap guy had called the state and somebody in Washington, D.C., about them catching all those dolphin.

The Marine Fisheries had Arnold and Billy Biggs out there on the beach at eleven o'clock that night looking for all those dolphin that we were supposed to have killed. Everyone that we killed was back behind the hills there. I told them, "You ain't gonna' find none on the beach. We didn't leave any on the beach. I can come over there and show you." They said, "No, the story is that you killed a lot of dolphin, like thirty or forty of 'em." I said, "Naw." He said, "Well we're gonna' be back up here in the morning, and the guys in the EPA in Washington are flying into Norfolk tonight and they are coming up here, too." I said, "What have I got into now?"

I go out there the next morning. We took the rig out there, and they're all out there so I explained what had happened. This guy that was head of the EPA was not much out of college I'd say. He said, "Well, we had information that y'all are trying to catch these dolphin to sell them to the Russians for $5,000 to $8,000 apiece." I looked at this guy and I said, "I tell you what sport, you tell me where I can sell 'em for $5,000 to $8,000 apiece, damn if me and the boys don't go to work. We're gonna' bury y'all behind the hills and go to work." I was just joking around there; it was so much BS. Arnold Daniels grabs me by the arm and drags me around behind the bow of the dory where he says, "Buddy, this guy ain't fooling with you. They can put you in jail over this. This guy's got a lot of power."

What come to pass, they were going to fine me $20,000 for each mammal that I killed. It was five of 'em behind the hills. In those days, we made pretty good money fishing, but not like that. A $100,000 fine, especially when we'd tried to release everything and got as many back alive in the ocean as we could.

I knew this fellow named Jim Need who'd been down here when we were rock fishing in the wintertime. He was head of the Sea Mammal Division of the Smithsonian Institute. I called him and explained what had happened, and he said, "Well, I'll send a guy down there. There has got to be something wrong with those dolphin. It's not normal for them to just stay inside of nets because they'll go out of it."

He sent Charlie Potter, who is head of the operation now (studying all these dolphin coming ashore now all down the East Coast). He sent him and a girl down here. We took them back there where they were. This was getting on about five or six days since they were caught, and we'd had a couple of hot days. We go back there, and they are pretty rank. There were a lot of maggots, but they go to work on them. They dissected them, cut 'em up right there and took their heads back with them.

Annie and I went up there to the Smithsonian just on a trip. I asked if I could talk to this guy Jim Need. I hadn't seen him in years. We were talking about this very episode, and he says, "Well, come with me. We've got a drawer back there with the inner ears out of the heads of those dolphin. What they had found was wrong with them was they had a parasite in their inner ear, and their sonar wasn't working. That was the reason we got 'em." He had contacted somebody that was over the guy that was going to prosecute me, and they dropped the charges against me.

It was funny to me that all this time (I've been married to Annie thirty-two years) that they still had those inner ears up there in the Smithsonian. Of all the years I've fished, that's the only time I ever killed a dolphin. Generally they'll go over the net unless they get down to where the water is shallow, then they'll go through it. One time we had a real heavy bunt they couldn't go through, and the guys went out there and just stood on the top line. There were a lot of fish in there, and they were just in there filling their bellies up. When they stood on the top line, they just went on out of there.

There was only one other time when we ever caught any. And then again when Joe Speight and I were doing some research for the State of North Carolina; we were working a nylon net against a monofilament net to see which was more deadly on mammals. We did catch a dolphin in that nylon net. My contention is that the nylon is worse than the monofilament because the mono springs back to the shape it's in, where nylon just wraps around anything that hits it, including you if you get in it; it will just wrap all over top of you. Not that I want to be caught in any net. If I was going to get caught in a net, I'd rather it be a mono net than a nylon net for that simple reason.

When I was dating Annie, the first time she ever came down here we had probably ten or twelve truckloads of bluefish. It was the first time she had ever seen a big haul. In fact, it was the first she had ever seen us haul to start with. I wasn't all the way divorced from Ellen. I still had a little going on my year after we had signed everything over.

Ellen was working for Charles Nunnemaker down at the packinghouse. We were still packing with Charlie. I used to hire everybody on the beach when I had a big haul to drive for us and off load. I was having Annie drive my truck with a load of fish on it. She had never driven a truck to start with before that. We kinda' had to explain how to shift those gears. Anyway, I sent this boy Charlie Robinson ahead of her and Bobby Romano that lives up the beach driving a load behind her. I knew it was going to kinda' get rough on Annie since she was dating me, and Ellen was working at the packinghouse. Charlie and Bobby were both pretty big boys, and I just told 'em when they left, "I know Annie is gonna' have to put up with some bad time as to mouth down there, but don't let it get out of hand." Bobby said, "Ah Buddy, we'll take care of it," so that went good.

Annie learned a lot about fishing from that day of swinging big bluefish. When we ended up, we had fifty-three thousand pounds that day. That was a lot of bluefish. They were the big bluefish. I think we had them up to sixteen, eighteen pounds that day. You don't see them much anymore.

TM: When I was running Monkey Island, "Hambone" [Ambrose Twiford] and I would ride down the beach picking up dunnage thrown from ships going into Hampton Roads to build duck blinds. This was before containers. We'd always take our rod and reels in case we ran up on a school of those big bluefish, and many times we would.

Talking about getting lumber to build duck blinds, when I built this house we used to go down the beach and pick up anything that would saw out a 2x4, 2x6 or 2x10. We set up a little ground mill here where we could saw

Annie Ponton unloading fish at Nunnemaker's fish house. *Annie Ponton.*

our own lumber. Most everything in this house came off the beach. The roof sheathing and flooring and all didn't come off the beach, but just about everything that it's framed with came off the beach; everything from wood from China to Spruce Pine from Canada. The only thing we didn't use was oak because it was so hard to drive nails in.

TM: I remember when we used to drive right over these hatch covers that had washed up on the beach. Then people started making expensive coffee tables out of them.

Oh yeah, we used to use them if we had a hole in the road that needed something over it we'd put a hatch cover over it. They were everywhere, and now they'd be worth a fortune.

TM: How long were your dories?

I built all my own boats. Mine were not like the ones the old guys built because we used plywood instead of planking them with juniper. We generally used oak ribs and cross pieces across the bottom and then plywood sides. The first one I built was eighteen feet. The lines of the first one we pretty much took off one of the old surf boats that they used during the old Life-Saving Service, but it wasn't as long as some of them. When you put a motor well in it, it wasn't big enough to carry much net.

I like a really high bow, and the more dories I built, and I probably built five or six of 'em over my running a fishing business, each one I'd make the bow a little higher. I like a bow that when I was taking a big sea I can hide behind it. The motor well was in the front so you could run the net out the back.

TM: What size outboard did you use?

When I started, I was using an old Mercury. The bad thing about those Mercurys (now, this is going back in the '60s or late '50s) is, when I'd get on that bar and you bust a few seas, the water will spray up the well and hit the back of those motors, and it would drown that bottom cylinder out on them Mercurys. Then I just lay there with one cylinder running. It wasn't enough power to push you on through there. After that had happened to me a couple of times, I'd catch a slack in the bar and come on back in and dry her out and try again. I got tired of that. One of the guys said the Evinrudes didn't drown out on the bottom cylinder. Then we started using 33hp Johnsons and Evinrudes. We had really good luck with them. The last one I used in that big dory was a fifty-horse Evinrude, and that worked real good.

Then we built a dory one time for just gill netting outside, and we put the well right in the stern, like a Simmons Sea Skiff is built, but it was just about eight foot wide in the stern. We put a 130-horse Evinrude on that, and that was the best sea boat I ever built.

We'd go along the beach, no matter how rough it was (I mean there is a limit), and we'd find like an out suck where we could go across those bars, and even if the bars were real shallow, that suck will have a little trough through that bar. We'd just launch in there and get it lined up on the beach. The guys hold her just right, and I could get that thing started and everybody would mount and we'd blast right on through. Then if you had a big rough coming on one of the outside bars, you could just turn and run right down the hollow between the two bars almost broadside, and then if you had a good wave gonna' catch you, just cut and run into it and then blast right on through it.

The craziest thing I ever did with that was: we set a bunch of gill nets for rock one night or one afternoon late right off Penny's Hill. I think we had seven nets set that night, and it was foggy the next morning. It had been rough the night before, but nothing you couldn't handle. That next morning, you couldn't see anything so we layed around the beach awhile. It got so you could see maybe fifty yards or so. You could see a little bit of the break. I said, "We know about where those nets are." They had those big orange buoys on them. I said, "If we just run due east we ought to run across them." We went ahead. When I went by the first buoy, those waves were still breaking. We went on out to the outside net we had and happened to run right in the buoy. We went

Unloading a dory off the trailer. *Annie Ponton.*

Going to sea in a dory. The crew is jumping in as they shove her off. *Annie Ponton.*

ahead and started working that net. By the time we got finished, it had right many fish. We got thinking about dropping on one of those inside nets when, all of a sudden, it cleared up, and we were in the wrong place. I'm thinking, "Man it's really looking tight in there." It was breaking all over our inside nets. That's where that 130 motor came in. We just picked a really big sea and got right in front of it, and we could outrun it. We actually had like one behind us and we were just laying in the trough, and we climbed right up on the back of that sea and just stayed right behind it; when it was breaking, you'd have to ease way off because you didn't want to run over top of it, but we come all the way to the beach on that one sea. We didn't go back to run the rest of those nets until the next day, when it was a lot flatter.

TM: How long was that dory?

It was twenty-five feet, but it was a lot wider than the others. Being wide, it would plane out real good. When we were having those winters when it was real cold and it iced up in the sound, we were long hauling in the sound and used that to pull net with. We were carrying a net skiff. Then we had a little hang boat that we took along with us.

We were out there one night after we'd fished all day, and we were running out of the backside of the landing strip over here (at the Whalehead Club) because there wasn't no water out of here. We had to break ice just out of that cut behind the airstrip. There was just a little channel going out to the black beacon, and then it was fairly open in the middle of the sound.

We were hauling up there on Great Shoal that day. We had roughly ten thousand pounds of catfish and perch. We were bailing fish until about eleven o'clock that night. We loaded that boat that we had the big motor on. We could carry about forty boxes in that. We had that full so we didn't have much freeboard in her, but there wasn't much wind chop. Then we loaded the bow of the net skiff. We probably had five thousand pounds in that. We had the net in the back and all the fish up forward. Then we had the hang boat, and we put about a thousand pounds in that.

When we were coming down the sound, the guys in the net skiff were still picking fish out of the bunt of the net and all the gilled perch we had and everything. The net skiff wanted to yaw because it was loaded so heavy in the bow, but the hang skiff being tied behind it helped to hold it straight.

It was about eleven o'clock when we left Great Shoal, and we were coming slow. I'd been married to Annie for not too long. She called everybody that she could get a phone number for on both sides of the sound because she was worried about us being out there. It never did get above freezing. We'd been working in ice all day, and it was making ice on the boat. She called Gene Austin. When we got right inside the black beacon, the only place to go back in was right where we had come out. Here comes Gene out in his skiff. Annie had called Shirley and Gene, and Gene said he'd run out there and see if he could run into us somewhere. When I got home I told Annie, I said, "Annie, if we do get overboard we are not going to last very long; the water is too cold." That really made her feel bad, you know. She was all upset, so I said, "Don't worry about it. We got three boats with us. If one sinks, we're gonna' go to another one, but it's nice to know your wife's concerned about you." She was just about ready to call the Coast Guard. I said, "Ah, don't do that Annie." It can be touch and go with the ice out there though.

TM: I love Currituck Sound and have been in it in some bad times both day and night, but I have always had great respect for it because I know how quick it can change. When there is ice in the sound, I try to stay out of the sound because I have seen what that ice will do. If it starts breaking up and moving, it is going to take everything with it, duck blinds or anything else that's in its way. I've tried to instill this in my grandsons, but I don't know if I'm getting through or not. Young folks think they know it all.

Sharks

We had a market for sharks one time with Billy Barcliff in Elizabeth City. We had a bunch of gear we were using for King Mackerel; six-inch real heavy mesh. It would hang those sharks and hold them. We would cut them right on the boat, just head and tail and gut 'em. Back in those days, for you to be able to sell the fins, they had to come off makos or thrasher sharks; they were worth something. Most everything we were getting were hammerheads and sandbars, maybe some bulls and stuff like that. The sandbars and bull sharks are classic-looking sharks. It's like everybody's picture of a shark.

The sand tigers are gray. They've got a really bad-looking mouth. They've got like needle-type teeth that just roll right out of their mouth, and there're lots of 'em. If that shark rubs up against you, it's gonna' cut you wide open.

When you get handling too much of anything, sometimes you get sloppy. My brother grabbed this little sandbar (they've got razor-sharp teeth), and he had him by the tail and was slinging him around trying to line him up on this board we had for cutting. That thing whipped around, and the top jaw got his arm. Man, he was bleeding like a stuck pig. We had right much more net to run. We took a handkerchief out of somebody's pocket (God knows it wasn't clean) and made a pressure bandage on it and tied it with a piece of sleeve of somebody's shirt and tied it across that wound, and he went right back to work. That bandage was pretty red when we finished.

Annie wanted to go out there with us one day to see what it was like gill netting outside. We had been catching mostly trout. It was in the spring of the year. We were up here just about where Macon Brock's house is. All of a sudden, the net starts leading right straight down. I was working the lead line, and another guy was working the top line. We were picking it up, and he could see there was something big in the net. It was a basking shark. Those things get up to about forty feet long. This one was probably somewhere in the low thirties. He was longer than the dory we were in, and he was still alive. We couldn't sell 'em. It was no good to us, so we wanted to release it alive, but it was all rolled up in the net. Nobody had said anything yet, and Annie hadn't seen it. I said, "Annie, if you want to see something, come over here." She looked over the side of the boat, and here's this shark that just goes on forever. We had the mouth right down there because we had the line running right across the mouth, and right where she was looking was a mouth that looked like you could put a bushel basket in it. That was the last time Annie went out in the boat with me. We got it all loose and sent him on his way.

One time we were trying to get on fish out there. A lot of times they will run in like a streak or in a certain depth of water. We weren't catching anything on the beach, so we were using gill nets. We'd set one net, and then we'd go set another outside of that. We'd come back and pick up the inside net, then take it outside and set it. We'd just keep going on out like that, just looking to see if we'd start picking up trout or croakers or anything. The trout was what we were looking for because they were pretty high. All of a sudden, we go back to pick up one inside net. We are out there about two miles. Both buoys are right together, and that's not a good sign; you know something's got in it. We start taking it up and all of a sudden, out there probably thirty feet, this tail comes out of the water. It's a whale, and this thing is just slashing the water. I'd say it's fifty feet long, and that dory was looking smaller all the time.

I told the boys, "Let's just let this on out, and we'll go around and pick up the other end and try to tow this thing close enough up to the beach before we untangle him. If he does turn us over, we can swim to the beach. We towed him in there to where we were about a quarter mile out. We weren't too far, so we start bringing it up. I had my brother, Gene Bichner, and Cuz in the boat. Gene couldn't swim until he went to work for the government pier down here, then he got his diver's license.

This thing is still trying to swim with us. When we had it up beside the boat, he's swimming a little bit and kinda' dragging us along. It's nothing really violent or anything. Gene gets his hand under the line, and all of a sudden the whale starts to roll, and when he does it pulls that line in Gene's hand down in the blubber on the whale and Gene starts to roll up on the back of the whale as he's rolling. Then Andy and Cuz got Gene by the leg trying to yank him loose from the whale. Gene is more on the whale than he is in the boat. We were all wearing gloves, and that glove comes off. The web goes with the whale, and Gene comes back in the boat.

Long story short, we got the whale loose, and he was going down tail first in the water. He was right off the stern of the boat, and there were three of the boys down at the stern. The whale just goes like he has gone out of sight. Then, all of a sudden, he was coming up right at the stern of the boat. He just headed right for the stern, and the guys were all running for the bow of the boat. All three of 'em were coming forward fast. The whale came out of the water about thirty feet off the stern and rolled off to one side, and that's the last we ever saw of him. When that fluke kicked he was *out of there. If he'd rammed the stern of that boat, we'd have had it. It's funny some of the things you can get into.*

TM: I tell you Buddy, you've been lucky.

Most days you're just fishing, but you have things happen every now and then over a period of time. I've enjoyed fishing. It's been good to me.

TM: How many years did you fish?

I would say the best of it was when I started in the early '60s until '85 to '89. One thing is they started making so many laws. It's like speckle trout. If you had a big haul of speckle trout, you couldn't have anything under twelve inches, and it was zero tolerance. Back in those days, we were catching a lot of speckle trout, and you had to have a man sitting there measuring speckle trout. You couldn't have undersize on the truck. When you are doing something in bulk, you need to have a tolerance like 5 percent, 10 percent or whatever. That's the way it had always been. You could have 10 percent undersize.

When they started going to zero tolerance on the stuff, there was no way we could keep up and still land big hauls. If you don't make the big hauls, you ain't gonna' make it. That's something I don't think the management people understand. They act like on the rockfish you can go out there everyday and say they allow you to have twenty fish a day. They act like you are going to be able to go everyday and get your twenty fish. It's not like a job. Fishing is a way of life. Even in the best years I ever saw, a lot of winters we wouldn't get the rock. We'd get short spurts of it.

This is a good example of the way it works: We hadn't hit any rock in three weeks. Junie Beasley called me one night and said they had hit a few down at Hatteras on the south point, so we went to Hatteras. He called me at 3:00 a.m. so he'd be down there before I got there. I got my crew together, and we got down there by around 8:00 a.m. We messed around there all day and made a couple hauls and caught nothing to amount to anything. We set up to make a haul on the south side of the inlet right at hard dark. That's back when you could haul both sides of the inlet and haul Cape Point. Junie had set up on the north side. He was gonna' haul the north point, and we were gonna' haul the south point. There were rigs set up all along there about dark because that's when they hit them was when it got dark.

We didn't have cellphones back in those days. If you had your front wheels in the water down there just south of Oregon Inlet, you could talk on a CB radio to about where Macon Brock's house is on Currituck Beach, which was north of Penny's Hill. You couldn't get much reception otherwise. My ex-wife (not ex at the time) was coming down the beach out of Virginia that day. There were two or three rigs fishing out there. I told her to see what they were doing when she came down the beach and told her what to do about getting the wheels in the wet sand. She called me and said the Belangia boys were at the Virginia line and they had four truckloads loaded with big rock and probably another truckload on the beach.

All my crew was standing there talking to a bunch of the other guys from other rigs. I didn't want everybody to know what was going on. I wanted to be the first one up there, so I just told my crew, "Come on, let's ride over there to the fishing center."

We started out of there and were going across the bridge, and Junie called me on the CB and said, "Buddy Ponton, is that you I see going over the bridge?" I said, "Yeah, Junie, that's me." He said, "What's going on? I thought you were going to haul on the south side?" I said, "Go north, young man, go north." He said, "For real?" I said, "Go north, go north." He said, "How far north?" I said, "As far north as you can go in North Carolina." He said, "We'll be right behind you, Buddy."

We got on the beach at Poyner's Hill and had to pull high water all the way up to the Virginia line (there were no roads on Currituck Beach at that time). There was a little bit of gravel down there at Ocean Sands, and we had to get through that. We got just south of the Virginia line and ran up with this boy Charlie Roberson, who had fished with me and lived at Carova Beach. His father, Robbie Roberson, ran a sport fishing boat out of Rudie Inlet. He was from Hatteras. I called him on the CB when I was going up there. We had another channel we talked to him on. As soon as I got him, I told him to switch over to the other channel. He said, "I've been trying to call you all day. There are the most rock you've ever seen up there on the line. I'm headed back toward Rudie, but they are right there on the line. They're so thick we're kicking them up with the prop on the boat."

When we got there, the Belangias were picking up net. They had five good truckloads of rock. We set out right there and hauled to the south. We had about three hundred boxes, thirty thousand pounds, in that haul. What I'm getting at is, when I said you get them in bunches, this is an example. We worked three days straight. We didn't take off time to sleep or anything else. If you got a nap, you got it while the net was being pulled around. The boys *shouldn't have been driving because they hadn't had any sleep for a right good while. The old sound road went from Pine Island to Duck along the sound. They'd get out of the truck and stick their head in the sound to wake up.*

When we got there, we hauled right then. We hauled at daylight the next morning. We made two more hauls that day, and then the rigs from Hatteras had heard about it and they came up here. Back in those days, there were a lot of rigs. There were even two rigs up there from Ocracoke. They had lined up for guys to take turns making that haul, so we weren't going to get that spot again for a while. We went up to the Virginia side of the line, and nobody was hauling that because the Virginia line was right there. It was dark, and I didn't think we were going to see anybody around there. We went ahead and hauled that. We had another big haul there. We worked three days, and I don't think we had a haul that was under five or six thousand pounds, and had as many as thirty thousand pounds. We did tear up a bunch of net because we got on a hang one time.

After that, the wind came out of the northeast, and we didn't see any more rock for a month, but we had pretty much made our season in three days.

Marine Fisheries doesn't seem to understand. Even in the best years we ever had, that was the way it worked. The next time you might see them, it might be Hatteras Inlet or somewhere like that.

TM: How about spot fishing?

This was a hot place for spots. If I heard on the fishing report they were catching spots down there around Lynnhaven and they were coming out of the bay, we could wait two days, and then we'd start hauling. It was just like clockwork. We'd hit 'em within two days. Sometimes it was a little faster, sometimes a little slower. Every north wind, we'd get another run. Croakers could be just about the same way. The problem with croakers was that if you hit the little ones, you had something you couldn't hardly sell and it took forever to pick 'em. I used to always tell the boys, "I like to catch fish I can hear hit the bed of the truck when I throw them in: big trout, big rock, big bluefish." Most guys didn't want to mess with big bluefish because they would tear the nets up so bad.

We made a seine that had a sixty-thread cod in it (a cod is the tail bag). I picked this up off the New York people who were rock fishing one time. I'm a certain believer in watching someone who has a better mousetrap. They were the first ones I ever saw with a cod in a seine, or a tail sack in a seine. It wasn't long before we had one on the rock nets, and we even used them on the spots at times. The trouble was with spots that if you couldn't get it out of the

Buddy Ponton, in white shirt, looking at a haul of spots. *Annie Ponton.*

Buddy Ponton and his and Annie's three children. *Author's collection.*

water, spots will wash bad and scale. It's hard to get your money out of 'em when they scale. Charles Nunnemaker had a cutting house he'd sell some to sometimes. A lot of times we'd get as much for them as the good-looking spot.

The net was made out of polypropylene, but it was sixty thread. It was like a quarter-inch twine. Then we had a feed that went into it that was reinforced with half-inch line that was twenty-one thread leading down into that cod, and then we had a double half-inch line on the top line and we had triple lead line. Once we got down to where we could pull on those five lines with the pulling straps, we put them around the whole thing and pulled with the trucks. We never broke anything. We have had as much as seventy-five thousand pounds in that net and never broke a thing. Now we couldn't get it out of the water, but we'd pull it ashore, and then we'd hook a loop in the very end of the tail bag because we had four half-inch lines that went down the tail bag to the end and they had eyes in them. We had a pulling strap, and when we put it all together to set it, it had a strap that went through the eye on those four lines. We hooked that to the truck, and we just pulled it around until it was like a big wall out in the edge of the ocean, and then we'd load everything we could. If the tide was coming in, we'd just keep loading on the high stuff, and then when the tide started to fall, we'd just go down that thing and we'd split it with a knife so we could pull it back.

A lot of times when we had big hauls, we had people come over and help us load and stuff like that. If it was Saturday or Sunday, a lot of the Currituckers from the mainland would be over here. We'd buy cases of different brands of beer. We had garbage cans out there we'd put beer and ice in. As long as you were helping load trucks or picking fish, you could drink all the beer you wanted. Once the word got out that we had a big haul, everybody knew we had beer and that worked great.

My accountant called me one time when I had all this beer on here as a business expense. He said, "Buddy, you can't list beer as a business expense." I told him what I was doing with it, and he said, "We'll try it." Folks would bring their family over. The kids would play on the sand dunes while they worked the nets; it was just a good time, and they all got a good mess of fish to go home with.

TM: Buddy, is there anybody fishing off the beach now?

There are a couple of guys that come up here and try it once in awhile. Everything we get now are proclamations that say what you can or can't do. Right now they've got one they put out that says you can't fish any monofilament within a hundred yards of the beach. They are doing it because they say somebody might catch a dolphin in a wade net. Travis, I've been in this a long time, and I've never seen a dolphin in a wade net.

It's because of all these dolphin that have been dying all up and down the East Coast from Jersey on south to Florida. It's supposed to be a virus.

Back in the '80s, they had a die-off too, but every dolphin that came ashore they were saying commercial fishermen were killing them all. If you start dragging piles and piles of dolphin ashore in nets, Salt Water Sportsmen *is going to have articles all over the front page about it, as well as other sport magazines. It just wasn't happening, but that didn't stop them from blaming it on commercial fishermen. I've told you today about every dolphin that I've ever caught. In the rock fishery, I only know of two or three that have ever been caught in recent history.*

But here's something else: it used to be that after spot fishing, you didn't see any more dolphin on the beach again until June. Now there are so many of them that I don't care whether you're in close to shore or you're outside on a trawler—they are everywhere. There are more of them than I've ever seen before in my life. This year I haven't seen as many. I was out there on the beach the other day (now this is cold weather), and they are knee deep out there. They must have gone by for two hours. If you have interaction with nets, sooner or later somebody's gonna' kill one.

TM: You were talking about wade nets a while ago. When I first started messing over here, Mr. Johnny Austin told me to get me a net thirty yards long. He said that's as far as you can wade out. That's what I did, and I've still got one. I'll probably never use it again.

I set wade nets if my family is coming down. We don't set the big seine now. It's hard to get a bunch of guys to go fishing now to set a big net, because nobody makes any money off of it anymore. Guys don't do this for free. The only reason I had a good crew and they stayed with me like they did was because we made money. I had no qualms about working men hard, but I never asked men to do anything I couldn't do. I had no qualms about 'em being tired. I've worked men until I've had them fall out on the sand picking fish. Nobody was complaining. On Friday they were getting really good money.

My brother and I have had other guys do this too. He took his share off one rock haul and bought a new 1971 Ford ¾-ton pickup truck with the share off one haul. It was like $3,700 for that truck. If you were paying guys the same money now, the same truck is probably $60,000. That's how far out our money system has gotten.

TM: That's like when I was selling oceanfront lots in Corolla for $12,000 in the 1970s. I wish I'd bought a bunch of them.

Ellen and I were lying in bed one morning. The weather had turned rough, and I'd given all the guys their checks the night before. I used to keep a bank account in Virginia and one in North Carolina because you couldn't tell which way the guys were gonna' go to cash their checks. When we hit rough weather, they were going to town somewhere. That morning, we got a call. It must have been about ten o'clock. Ellen took the call. She said, "This woman is with Virginia National Bank and says there are two guys there that have checks for over $4,000, and they want cash and they are barefooted and don't smell very good." I took the phone, and she related the same sentence to me. She said, "They look kinda' dirty and they don't smell good." I said, "What's the name on the check?" She told me and I said, "Pay them." She said, "Pay them?" I said, "Pay them. They earned it." It's crazy. I could just see 'em walking in there barefooted.

When we went to Wrightsville Beach mullet fishing, I used to trade with First Union in Dare County. They knew how my crew was; I or my wife would be depositing money, and they would be at another teller cashing their checks.

I talked to whoever was managing the bank in Dare County and asked him if there was any way he could clear a way for me with First Union in Wrightsville Beach. I said, "You know how we operate. We may be putting money in one place and they'll be taking it out another, but I'll always have everything covered." He said he'd make some phone calls. When we first went down there, we deposited some money to open an account. The first big haul we had (and that was right away), they didn't know me from Adam except that I'd been recommended. My wife and I are depositing the check, and the boys are drawing it out at another window. They were barefooted and didn't smell too good!

I believe in hard work.

There is something else we perfected. When we first came down here, when folks would make a haul, they had a man with a Danforth anchor or either a big ell head anchor that was working the bunt. We tied off to that thing. When you are fishing in the ocean, the net moves all the time; it's very rare you ever haul back in the same place. When we would haul, they had this guy with this anchor. The net goes out, hopefully around the fish, and you pull this end with a truck. The bunt keeps working toward where you're pulling the wing in. He'd keep jumping this anchor down. When we started using longer nets, sometimes that guy working the bunt of the net is trying to drag the anchor man right on to sea, particularly if you go across a big out suck. That anchor will start plowing.

I was thinking about this one day, so I said, "I'm just going to hook it to the truck." We quit using the anchor. We'd just hook it to the truck because a man could handle the truck. I have had them try to drag the truck around sideways before, but I never had it where I thought I was going to lose the truck.

When we started doing that, all these guys said, "Man, you're gonna' dump every haul you get. Ain't no way you'll ever land a fish like that." Well, within two years I guarantee there wasn't anybody on this beach that wasn't fishing the bunt with a truck. What we'd do when we got a big haul, see when you're hauling with a truck down here and just a man on an anchor you couldn't get that slide. You could slide ten thousand pounds and sometimes more than that on good beach, you could slide it right out high and dry. It's just like the theory of a skim board. You get that thing sliding, and the water gets underneath it and it'll slide right on that little thin layer of water. Just like hydroplaning. As long as you don't stop, it'll keep coming. You see you can't do that when you're just pulling one side. What we'd do when we started using the bag was we'd get that thing all set up. Both trucks would go way down in the water as far as they could and get a low hookup. Then we'd get a big sea hit that thing, and we'd start going. You don't want to go really fast. You just want to keep it moving. Just keep sliding it. With trucks you can bring that net right on out of the water. That was the best thing I ever did for a big haul.

You learn things as you go along. I was green when I started, but I always liked the fishing.

Someday somebody might want to know how it worked to fish off the beach. Buddy has described it in detail.

PART III
HUNTING AND FISHING LODGE ON MAINLAND CURRITUCK

CAROLAND FARM

There were several hunting lodges in Currituck that were just peoples' homes. They would have duck hunters come, and they would provide room and board and guides. I'm not going to try to name them because I'd be sure to leave some out.

In one of my other books, I told about the Barnes and Williams Lodges on Knott's Island. In another of my books, I told Mary Wright's story about their hunting lodge. The Wrights' lodge was in earlier years.

Now I'm going to give you the history of what was the most well-known hunting and fishing lodge on mainland Currituck, starting in 1957 and closing in 1992: Caroland Farm, operated by Colon and Dorothy Grandy.

In all my other books, I've talked about duck hunting in Currituck, but I haven't said much about the bass fishing. From the 1960s to the late 1970s, bass fishing was as big an industry as duck hunting in Currituck. During that time, the sound was full of milfoil (a type of grass). It was so thick we had paths where we ran boats all across the sound. You had to have a two-blade weedless wheel on a gas boat to get through it.

Currituck Sound was written up in *Sports Afield Magazine* as being the largest largemouth bass hatchery in the world. They said the grass was so

Hunting and Fishing Lodge on Mainland Currituck

Above: Caroland Farm Lodge. *Dorothy Grandy.*

Left: Colon and Dorothy Grandy. *Dorothy Grandy.*

HAND-CRAFTED BOATS OF OLD CURRITUCK

Left: Sportsman and guide Bud Lupton. *Dorothy Grandy.*

Below, left: Sportsman with large bass caught in Currituck Sound. *Dorothy Grandy.*

Below, right: Sportsman with bass caught on a flyrod in Currituck Sound. *Dorothy Grandy.*

thick the little fingerlings could hide in the grass and not be seen and eaten by other fish.

Ambrose "Hambone" Twiford, a well-known guide, told me he'd had sportsmen catch 175 bass in one day. Of course, they had to throw back all but 8 per man, which was the limit. This was in the days before the fast bass boats with all the electronics they have today. People came to Currituck to bass fish like they had done since the late 1800s to duck hunt. They would hire local

Hunting and Fishing Lodge on Mainland Currituck

Sportsman with guide Elmer Merrell, poling him in Currituck Sound. *Dorothy Grandy.*

guides to pole them around the marshes and ponds to cast for largemouth bass. People don't hire guides to pole them around Currituck Sound anymore to cast for bass. Now they have these fast bass boats with all kinds of electronics, but I don't think they can find the fish like the local people.

People, including me, fussed about the milfoil when it was here because it was hard to get through with a boat, plus it would wash up on the shore and stink. Nobody knows why it came or left, but it left like it came; when it left, the bass went with it.

Miss Carrie Walker was a schoolteacher in Currituck for many years. She had a large home in Poplar Branch and would take in hunters and fishermen. She taught me in the second grade at Currituck School, which is now J.P. Knapp Junior College.

Miss Carrie knew Colon and Dorothy Grandy, a young couple that hadn't been married long. Colon was farming with his daddy, and Miss Carrie knew he was a hard worker who knew a lot about hunting and fishing from growing up here. The following is quoted from Dorothy:

In 1957, Colon and I were approached by Miss Carrie Walker....She knew we were just starting out in life and needed to work. Colon was farming with his daddy and didn't have much income. Colon and I talked it over as we were living in a small home across the road from the lodge and we had Colon Jr. We were young and Miss Walker said, "If you will work, I think it will be good for you." Miss Carrie told us to just keep the place up and pay the taxes. She and Mr. Walker were both fixing to move to Charlotte, North Carolina. Their only daughter, Carolyn, lived there. Colon and I laughed and said we would try it for a year. I had no experience in running a lodge. That one year turned into 35 years, but common sense and treating people like you wanted to be treated worked for us. We were very fortunate to have good help. I'll soon tell you about them. Colon had a very good personality and could get along with anyone. He had good blinds and was able to get good guides. It didn't take too long before people started to come. My part of the job was to put good, delicious meals on the table, keep the lodge clean and in good order, the lawn neat and, of course, a whole lot more. This included book keeping, buying groceries, and taking care of the needs of the guests. The guests told us what they wanted and we listened. There was also taking good care of our little boy, Colon Jr.

The help we had at the lodge was incredible. First it was Roberta and Augustus Saunders. They helped us move in on September 1st, 1957. It was a hot day. Mrs. Walker had left it very nice, but we wanted everything polished and washed. We had some furniture that we moved in to replace what Mrs. Walker had taken with her. I asked Colon if he had any money so I could buy a few things that we needed. He said, "I can let you have $100.00 and that's all. I just don't have much." I said, "Okay, I'll make do." I bought a rug for the living room, some drapery material for the windows, and a set of china. We were in business.

That afternoon, Colon and Augustus were laughing. I asked Roberta what was so funny. She laughed and said, "I think they found a bottle with some bourbon in it."

Soon there was a knock on the door. It was our first guest, a man visiting someone in the area who just wanted a place to stay. His name was Joseph Jauph.

It was getting close to the hunting season. Colon was getting the boats and blinds ready. I didn't know too much about running the lodge, but my mom told me, "Give them good meat, potatoes and bread, and good homemade pies and they will come back."

My mom and dad had some experience with hunters early in life. In fact, I still have a very pretty bowl that one of the hunters who came to Bell's Island gave to my mother.

We had fine help at the lodge. I mentioned Roberta. Then there was Mary Dunston and Ruth Gallop. Both of them had worked at Swan Island Club.

Hunting and Fishing Lodge on Mainland Currituck

Top: Colon Grandy in a duck blind on the marsh in Currituck Sound. *Dorothy Grandy.*

Left: Billy Grandy with his dog and Bell Jones, the cook. *Dorothy Grandy.*

They were so good. Over the years, there were Bell Jones, Rona Saunders, Marie Simmons, Sarah Saunders, Miss Estelle Lane, Janice Beasley, and Miss Ann Brickhouse. We all worked together and made it work.

As years went by, Colon Jr. and Billy (our younger son) pitched in, especially on Sunday. That was change-over day. They stripped beds and vacuumed. We had to get ready for a new group.

After about five years, Colon took a job with North Carolina Marine Fisheries, a job he kept for 28 years. That meant I had to assume more responsibility. He had to be away from time to time to go to schools and his job. His job covered a big territory of 13 counties.

About the same time he took that job, a fellow by the name of Joel Arrerington had a job of travel and promotion. He was able to bring writers to our lodge. This made it possible to get a lot of advertisement in magazines such as Field & Stream, North Carolina Wildlife, The Baltimore Sun, and many others.

When I was expecting our second son, Billy, I told Colon we had to give up the lodge because I couldn't keep a baby there and the guests might not want a baby there. About this time, an article came out in the paper saying that Farmers Home was lending money to farmers at a low interest rate. Colon was still farming, so instead of giving up the lodge, we built a brick ranch home across the road. Then we had two sons, two homes, two yards, and more work than ever, but we were young and in good health so we just did what needed to be done.

Also my grandmother, mom, and dad needed some help. I managed that, too. The bass season ran from about April to the end of June, then from September 1st through October. The waterfowl season ran from November through part of January. We had some breaks, but there was always something to do with upkeep on the lodge. We had a really good friend, Vernon Douglass, who could do everything. On weekends when he was away from his job, he helped us so much. He was a nice man. Colon and I both liked him and we liked his wife, Irene, as well. She would help us, too, when we needed her. They were good home folks.

These were some of the menus I served: on Sunday nights, I served prime rib roast, potatoes, collard greens, stewed tomatoes, corn bread, biscuits, gravy, and complementary wine. Cherries jubilee was served as dessert from a silver chafing dish with the lights dimmed.

Over the years, I was encouraged to start a rose garden by some of the guests. I would have a silver bowl with roses for a center piece on the table. Some of my friends would say, "Dorothy, why do all that for men?" I said, "I think they like it too." The table was always set with white starched cloths, dinner with cloth napkins. Anyway, the fellows came back year after year and always commented on how nice things were.

Monday nights, I served seafood, like fried flounder. In the hunting season, the first course was an oyster roast in a building out back. Then the flounder, French fries, tossed salad, corn bread and biscuits; dessert was lime or orange sherbet with cream de menthe, if desired, and cookies.

On Tuesday nights I'd serve fried chicken, creamed potatoes with butter beans or string beans, tossed salad, and biscuits and gravy. Dessert was apple pie with vanilla ice cream or, in season, strawberry short cake and whipped cream.

Wednesday was change-over day. Sometimes we had roast turkey, oyster and plain dressing with gravy, creamed potatoes, candied sweet potatoes,

Hunting and Fishing Lodge on Mainland Currituck

Top: Guests enjoying one of Dorothy's meals. *Dorothy Grandy.*

Left: Bud Lupton, guide, with two sportsmen and geese. *Dorothy Grandy.*

collards or snap beans, biscuits, homemade cranberry sauce, and pumpkin pie with whipped cream.

Breakfast was ham or sausage, bacon, fried eggs, scrambled eggs, cheese and buttered grits, toast, biscuits, two or three kinds of preserves, two or three kinds of juices, and coffee.

Then there were always the packed lunches. Baked ham sandwiches, always homemade cake (pound cake, fresh apple cake, or walnut cake). Orders for the thermoses were taken the night before.

We were known for great meals. People would say, "Do we have to fish or hunt? Can't we just come here to eat?"

Breakfast had to be served early and lunches packed early. My day started at around 3:30 a.m. The guides were ready around 6:30 or 7:00 a.m. Then we'd clean up the kitchen and dishes, make the beds, and go over the whole lodge.

One time some older men were here from up north. The sound had frozen up and they didn't want to go hunting so they stayed in and played cards. Ruth Gallop and I made a pot of soup from a country ham. Ruth and Mary Dunston had both worked at Swan Island and they taught me a lot. The bone was left with the meat on it. I served the fellows a bowl of it to go with their sandwiches. Ruth and I left to go to the store and post office. To our surprise, when we came back the soup was gone. They had gone in the kitchen and helped themselves and asked if I could make another pot. I said no because I didn't have another ham bone. They liked it and that was all that mattered.

We got our supplies from Elizabeth City. We would go to A&P grocery store, Globe Fish Company, and the Freezer Locker (they cut the meat, seasoned it, and tied it up). Then it was back to the lodge, to unpack everything and put it up. Soon it would be time to start dinner.

We would have the guests' ice buckets filled, glasses in their rooms, and a few things for them to snack on, like cheese, crackers, and nuts. The lodge was nice and warm. They said it was their home away from home.

The game the sportsmen killed had to be cleaned and packed for them. We had help to do this. We had an ice house out back where we kept it until they were ready to go home. Everyone had their name on their game. They said when they got home they'd freeze it, then they'd all get together and have a wildfowl dinner. This was the same thing with the fish.

SPORTSMAN'S VIEW, BY PURCELL KIMSEY

Now I'm going to present what a sportsman wrote about staying at Caroland Farm and hunting from there. Dorothy showed me this piece that one of their guests, Purcell Kimsey, had written. I decided the best way for you to know what it was like to hunt at Caroland Farm was to let somebody who had hunted there tell you (with some editing done by RM). I give full credit to Purcell Kimsey for the following.

Hunting and Fishing Lodge on Mainland Currituck

Duck Hunting on Currituck Sound and Staying at Caroland Farm
by Purcell Kimsey

Bud Lupton was our first guide. Doug Howard and I were at the lodge, where we always put all the guides names in a hat and everyone would reach in and pick out a name. Doug and I had picked Bud Lupton; we didn't know who he was.

All duck hunters liked to go down to the docks, where the hunters were coming in with their day's hunt. While we were standing near the docks, we heard a loud roar of a car coming down the road coming straight for the docks. This car ran within ten feet of going into the sound; he put on his breaks and slid within three feet of the water. The driver opened the door of the car and fell out on the ground. Doug asked, "Who in the world is that?!?" The answer came, "That is Bud Lupton, your guide for tomorrow. He'll be fine by then."

Early the next morning here comes Bud, sober and ready to go. He had a large bottle of Pepto Bismol, which he was drinking like water. He had had a bad day, but he was a very good guide. He could call ducks and geese with his mouth without a duck call. Doug and I had a good day of shooting. When one duck

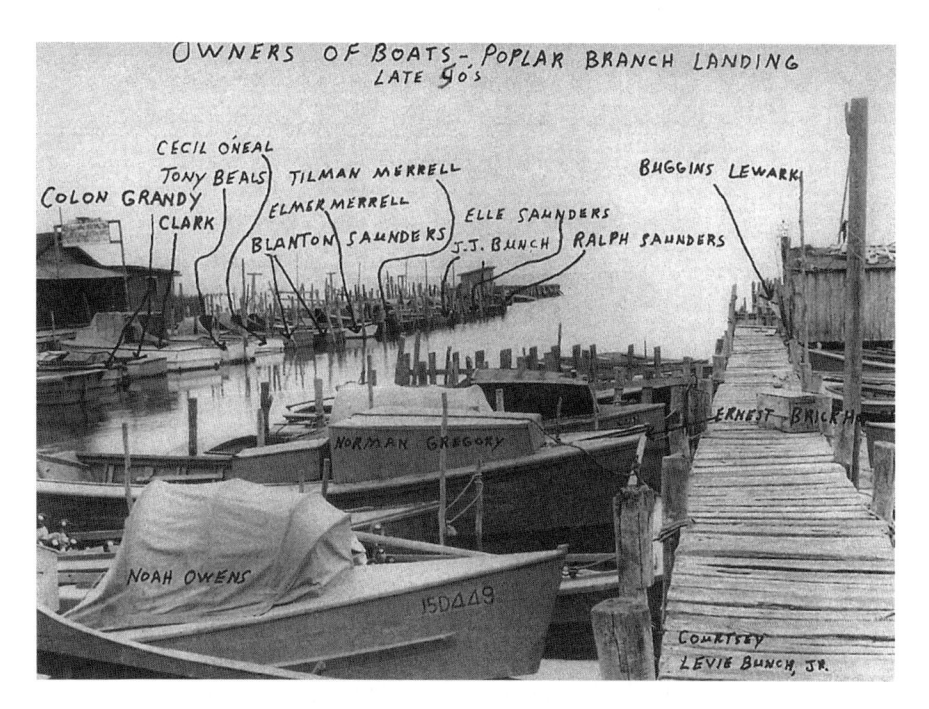

Poplar Branch Landing with boat owners' names in the 1950s. *Levie Bunch Jr.*

111

flew by, we both shot at it three times each; that duck just looked at us and kept on flying. He flew about a 100 yards, turned around and came back. We each shot three more shots and the duck kept on flying. Bud laughed and said, "You fellows can't hit a barn door." I said, "Well, here he comes again, you shoot this time." Bud shot three times and the duck kept on going. Bud said, "That duck sure can carry a lot of lead!" It was a very windy day and our shot were blown so badly we would miss. We had shot at ducks all day and only hit a few. We had not seen a goose. The day was about over and the wind had calmed down. The guide had gone after his large boat. I said, "Doug, here comes a lone goose." It was a perfect distance for a perfect shot. We both shot three times and the goose kept flying. I said, "Doug, it's not the wind." That day was lots of fun and a beautiful day. Doug Howard was my brother-in-law, a great fellow. In those days, around 1960, we had great times. I can remember Author Dickens, who owned Dickens Insurance Company. One day I was hunting in a marsh blind and Author and his partner were hunting what we called an open water blind, which was out on the sound. All day long we saw ducks fly by their blind. The shooting sounded like a little war. We thought they would have their limit of ducks. When we went in to the docks, we asked to see their ducks. They had only two small ducks. The guide said Author shot one foot to the left of everything all day. After that, Author's name was "one foot to the left."

In those early days as we would leave the dock in the early morning, the sky would be full of all kinds of ducks, geese, and swan. As we left the dock, on our left was a duck reserve. It was always full of all kinds of ducks. I always wondered how the ducks knew it was a reserve. Boats were not allowed to go through this area, but we would go along the side of the reserve, which had only a few floats to show the area. When we went by they would not fly; they knew they were safe.

The old docks and buildings where we would meet the guides with their boats for the day's hunt were very picturesque, especially early in the morning with Currituck Sound in the background. In later years, the Wildlife Commission tore down all the old buildings and docks. They built new ones which are not nearly as picturesque as the old ones.

Ed Grimsley in his younger years had lived in the northeastern part of North Carolina and loved it. Ed started this group of hunters going to Caroland Farm Hunt Club. At all our meals Ed always sat at the head of this long table which would hold 10 people. We called Ed "Big Daddy."

The Caroland Farm house was a large two floor house with four bedrooms and a bath upstairs. There were two bedrooms, one bath, living room, dining room, kitchen, and two screened in porches downstairs. One porch was on the side and went all around to the front. There was a side drive for several cars.

Hunting and Fishing Lodge on Mainland Currituck

Top: The oyster house, with Colon Grandy Jr., Warren Lupton (he was a federal game warden) and General Turnage. *Dorothy Grandy.*

Left: On the left is General Turnage. On the far right is Colon Grandy Sr. Note the old crosscut saws hanging on the wall. *Dorothy Grandy.*

The lodge was about 100 feet from the road with large shrubs. The back yard had several out buildings, one which we used for our oyster outings. There was a field back of the house that was about 400 feet wide and 1000 feet deep. It went back to a small pond. It was usually full of ducks. Along the side of the field was a row of trees and small bushes.

When we arrived at the lodge early the first day, or when we had our limit of ducks for the day, we would go quail hunting. One morning I looked out the back window at the field and it was full of snow geese. There must have been several thousand. All of us hunters could have gotten our limit, which was five snow geese each, but not any of us would fire a shot.

In later years, the Grandys added a new large bath which was half way between the first and second floors. The Grandys lived in the lodge the first few years. Later they built a fine new brick home across the street.

Our duck hunt started in High Point, North Carolina. As soon as the duck season was set, Dorothy would call me, so we always had the first weekend of the duck season. We started sending out cards to the hunters for them to send in a deposit for that date; first come, first on the list.

A few days before the hunt, we checked our guns and gear to be sure everything was in good shape. We would meet and decide how we would car pool. We would all leave High Point around 10:30 a.m. and go up I-95 to just this side of the Virginia border, where we picked up highway 158. When we got to Roanoke Rapids, it was a good time to eat lunch. We would meet at the same restaurant, which was just on the other side of highway I-95.

Some years later, we all stopped at this spot, but the restaurant had burned. We stayed on 158 and our next stop was Winton. All there was in this town was an ABC store, which was run by one woman. We wanted to get a bottle of something to drink. We needed this when we got in from a long day of hunting. We went through Elizabeth City, then out toward Currituck Sound. A few miles before 158 turned south along the sound on our left was a small airport that was used in World War II. This is where Carson Stout landed his small airplane. Doug Howard would fly down with Carson. Carson had been mayor of High Point. We would continue down route 158 to route #3, turn left and go to the end of the road, turn right, go about one block, turn left into the drive, and we had arrived.

We took our luggage up to our rooms. My room was upstairs and my bed was in the outside corner. I slept in the same bed every year that I hunted. Back in the early 1960s our hunting trip was in November, about two weeks before Thanksgiving. The hunting season got shorter and shorter. Now the season starts just before Christmas and the limits are very low. The first evening, we would sit in the parlor, where there was a bowl of mixed nuts, a bucket of ice and mixes for any kind of drink. We had our own bottle. We would shoot the bull about last year's hunt and other events. Then at about 6:30 p.m. the dinner bell would ring. We all had our own seats. Ed Grimsley was at the head of the table. I was the first chair to his left, Judd Sherman was beside me, and across from me was Bill Morris. Judd was a Yankee. I should say, "Damn" Yankee. He came south years ago and will not leave.

I'm not going into the food because Dorothy has already told you about that.

When we had all finished dinner, we would have the drawing to see who would hunt with which guide. We took the guides names and made two

Hunting and Fishing Lodge on Mainland Currituck

Boats waiting to pick up sportsmen from: Mr. John Poyner—Superintendent of Currituck Club; Pine Island Club; Whalehead Club; Currituck Club

Poplar Branch Landing in the late 1950s. The two men working on the motor in the boat are Howard Sumrell and Otto Bateman. *Levie Bunch Jr.*

slips of paper with his name on them. We put all these names in my leather hat (I had bought this hat in Mexico about 1954 and it was my lucky hat). Each hunter would reach in and pick one name. This is the guide he would hunt with the first day. The second day we would do the same thing, except we would look at the name as it was pulled out. If it was the same guide we had the day before, we would put it back in the hat and draw again. We thought this was the fairest way to select our guides.

Some hunts I have been on, the ones who got up the hunt always got the best blinds and guides. I never thought that was fair. After the drawing, Ed Grimsley would say, "Let's go for a walk." We would walk down the road toward the docks. There was an old country store just this side of the docks (Mr. Jerry Bunch's store. In the 1940s and '50s, he furnished much of the groceries and supplies for Whalehead, Currituck, and Pine Island Clubs. They all picked up their members and their guests at Poplar Branch Landing in boats.) We would go in and browse around. They had shot gun shells and all kinds of hunting gear.

After this, we walked to the docks and looked out on Currituck Sound. The air was brisk and cold. All the boats were rocking with the wind and waves. We then walked back to the lodge, which was about a mile. It would not be long before we all started to bed. I would be one of the first. When everyone was asleep the snoring was like a frog pond. One night there was a new hunter in my room. I woke during the night and heard this noise. It sounded like an old piston well pump. I got up and went in the hall, then I listened at the bathroom door. I turned and saw it was coming from my room. I went back in the room and listened. I saw it was coming from a bed across the room. I have heard a lot of snoring, but this was the strangest I have ever heard.

When we went to the duck blinds, we went by boat. The boats were about 24 feet long with an outboard motor. We would get in the front of the boat and the guide would pull a canvas top (hood) up which covered about half the boat. This kept the cold wind and water off the hunters. The guide stood in the stern of the boat so he could run the motor and see where he was going. He always wore a wet suit. Sometimes it would take 30 minutes to get to the blind. Sometimes the boat had to break ice to get to the blind.

One cold morning, Dr. Gray and I drew Watson Stuart for our guide. He had a float blind. Float blinds have a rack, which goes all around the boat. It is flat on top with holes drilled in the top so pine limbs or branches can be inserted. This makes a blind that floats on the water around the boat. The ducks cannot see the hunters or the boat. It was a cold morning with ice all around. I got in the boat. I started to tell Sy about the ice on the edge of the boat, but before I could say anything, he stepped on the ice and his feet went out from under him. He fell hard and his side hit the stern of the boat. He fell so hard that it almost sank the boat. His glasses went in the water. He just laid there. I reached in the water, got his glasses, and said, "Sy, I think we should take you to the hospital. You're bound to have some broken ribs." Sy said, "Just let me lay here a minute and rest, then we'll go hunting." In a few minutes we pulled out from the dock and headed for the float blind, which was already in place. This was the best hunt either of us ever had. We had three ducks on the water at one time. The wind was blowing hard, taking the fallen ducks away from the blind. Watson had this big Chesapeake retriever whose name was Big Red. Watson said "fetch" and Big Red jumped in the ice cold water and started after the downed ducks. He got the first duck, looked at it and swam to the second duck, looked at it and swam to the third and last duck which was a good 150 yards from the blind, because the wind was so strong. Big red picked up this duck, swam back picked up the second duck, then he came to the first duck. He had trouble getting all three in his large mouth, but he brought all three back to the blind. Later that day I shot a duck, he hit the water, but was not dead. Big Red jumped in the water and swam after the duck. The duck went under the water. Big Red went under after him. I was looking at the duck as he swam by the boat about two feet under the water, Big Red was swimming right behind him. He finally caught the duck. Big Red was one of the finest retrievers I have ever seen.

By the time we were ready to call it a day, Sy was in bad shape. Later, when we were home, an x-ray showed Sy had six cracked ribs.

One extra cold morning when I was hunting with Watson and Big Red, ice was all around the blind. When we shot a duck it would fall on the ice. Big Red would go after the duck and when he got to the ice he would jump up and come down with his front feet and break the ice till he got to the duck. Then he'd bring it back to the blind. [I can't help inserting that I've seen my grandson Chandler Sawyer's Chesapeake, "Chief," do the exact same thing in the ice this year. Sorry for the interruption.—TM] Watson would reach down and help Big Red out of the cold water and into the boat. Big Red always shook off the cold water. He would sit and watch for ducks while Watson was eating a sandwich. He would look at the food but would not take it until Watson said, "Eat."

One cold foggy morning, Paul Snipes and I were in a float blind. There was about an inch of ice on most of the sound. Some ducks came through the fog and Paul pulled up his gun and shot. I said, "What in the world are you shooting out of that thing?" It looked like a missile. He had shot the modifier off the end of his gun. It went up and came down on the ice, slid about 75 yards on the ice, then came to a broken place in the ice and went in the sound.

When we first started hunting at Caroland Farms, the blinds were so poorly built, it was like sitting outside. I started taking a large gas heater with me. All the guides and hunters laughed at me. I could heat the blind plus we could heat our sandwiches. After the second year, all the fellows wanted to hunt with me. The blinds were built much better in later years, and all the hunters got gas heaters to keep them warm. One nice duck day when I was hunting with Paul Snipes, the heater was on and the blind was nice and warm. I was over in the corner of the blind, got sleepy and went to sleep. Paul slipped my shotgun and slipped a dud in the second shell. We had our limit of birds except for two. Paul punched me and said, "Here they come on your side." I jumped up and shot one duck and had a perfect shot at another. The gun just made a click, so the duck flew by. Our guide got so mad at Paul, he made an ass of himself. We had our limit except for one. The guide wanted to take us to the lodge and call it a day; it was about 10:00 a.m. I laughed about the whole thing. About that time in came some ducks and we got our limit. The guide said, "Let's go in. We have our limit." I said, "We don't have our limit on geese." "But geese don't come to this blind," he said. I replied, "They might; also it's a beautiful day. Let's just enjoy it." We watched ducks fly all day. There were no geese, but we stayed until it was time to go in. I found out later why the guide wanted to go in early. He had this girlfriend whose husband worked all day. The guide was later found dead; they say it was suicide, but who knows.

In the 1960s and '70s, we would sit in the duck blinds, look over on the beach near Corolla Lighthouse at the large sand dunes. They would be covered with Canada geese. They looked like a bunch of turkeys. One early morning, Harlon Burton and I were in a marsh duck blind. We were about 2000 yards from the duck reserve. I said, "Harlon look, here comes six Canada geese. They're low and coming right at us." We stayed low as the geese got close. I said, "Harlon, you start from the back and I'll start from the front." We got all six, one fell in the blind; I had to duck to keep from another hitting me in the head, and this was our limit for the day. Later in the afternoon, we saw a flock of ducks coming from our right. There were so many of them we would not shoot at the flock, we each would pick out a duck to one side. This was such a large flock of ducks, they flew by us for 45 minutes. I shot 20 times and got 20 ducks, Harlon said he shot 20 times. When the guide picked up the ducks there were 40 ducks, which was the limit on that duck. [They must have been Coot; Blue Peters.—TM]

One day I was hunting with Rosco Adams; he was the executive vice president of Wachovia Bank of High Point and had only hunted a few times. It was very cold that day and we had plenty of ducks come into our decoys. I would say, "Rosco, you get the ones on your side and I'll get the ones on mine." He shot and shot, but was not having much luck. There was a blind about 500 yards to our left. The geese were going to their decoys all day. At times there would be six go in and six would leave. I didn't know who was in that blind. They couldn't hit them. This went on most of the day. Rosco wanted to know why they all went to that blind and not ours. I laughed and said, "They know they're safe." I said, "We'll be patient and some will come our way." Finally, as some started to the other blind, we started our goose call and they headed our way; they came in perfect and started to land in our decoys. I said, "Let's get them. We stood up and each fired three shots and all three fell right in front of us. I said, "Rosco, that was good shooting." Years later Rosco would say that was the prettiest sight he had ever seen.

Hunting and Fishing Lodge on Mainland Currituck

We had lots of cold blustery mornings. I remember ice was all over the sound, especially around the edges; the small ponds behind our blind were frozen solid. Across the sound to our left about 500 yards, was another blind in which Carson Stout was hunting. There was a lot of shooting. I hoped they were getting a lot of duck. Carson had bad circulation in his legs and feet and he got so cold his group went to the lodge. This was a very good day for hunting duck. The wind was blowing about 20 miles an hour and the ducks were flying very fast and close to the water. In those conditions, you had to lead them (shoot ahead of where they were) at least six feet and you would hit very few. I went out a trail behind our blind that led to a small pond. There was a small hole in the ice, about 10 feet round. The ducks were trying to get in this hole. Most of the ducks were mallard and black ducks. They would come down to land and hit the ice and slide 25 to 50 feet. I shot two ducks at different times. They were 100 feet in the air and when they fell they hit the ice and would bounce about six feet in the air. You would think they were dead. In a few minutes they would get up and fly off. I had to shoot them again.

One day I was hunting with Jack Rives in Gilbert Brickhouse's blind. Gilbert had this ten gauge double barrel shotgun and was bragging on how good he was hitting ducks with it. Gilbert said that his blind was a duck blind, no geese ever came to his blind. We'd been hunting for about an hour when I said, "Gilbert, isn't that two geese?" They were about 1500 yards in front of us, and heading south. He said, "Yes, they're geese, but it wouldn't be any use calling them; they're too far away." I started calling anyway and those geese turned and started coming our way. I said, "Jack, you and Gilbert get ready; they're coming straight for us. You do the shooting, I'll keep calling." The geese came straight in front of us and were about ten feet over our heads. Jack and Gilbert emptied their guns, but the geese kept going. I asked them if they could have had a better shot and they said, "No." I said, "Gilbert, I'll call in another goose. Then I'll do the shooting." We sat there about an hour. I said, "Jack, do you hear a goose calling?" "I think I do," he said. I started my goose call. Sure enough, the goose answered. I kept calling and then we saw a lone goose headed for our blind. I told them not to shoot. I said this was my goose. He came straight for us. We stayed down so he couldn't see us. When he got in range, I stood up, shot one time and the goose was dead.

Gilbert said, "I want that goose caller. I'll give you a pair of mated mallard ducks for the caller." We made a deal. I said, "Gilbert, it's not as much the caller as it is how you use it." I learned by talking to geese on a small pond on my farm out of High Point. I had bought a pair of Canada geese in Poplar Branch a few years before and they'd raised six young geese. With this caller I could talk to the geese and they'd talk back. They'd fly over and land in this small pond.

Through the years we had seen the Swan population double and triple. There was a $1,000.00 fine for having one and they'd take your gun if you shot a swan; if you had a swan in your car, sometimes they took the car. The guide said that a swan was better to eat than a turkey.

One guide said if you shot a swan, he would spread out like a white sheet on the water, all the time calling out, "Warden, warden, warden!" Now there are so many swan, the Wildlife Commission has started issuing approximately 6,000 permits a year for the shooting of swan. The first year, I had a permit to shoot a swan. The day was almost over and I had not shot a swan. We looked up when we heard swans calling. There was a long line of them, but they were very high right over our head. I took my Winchester, which had a long fiberglass barrel. I waited until they were straight overhead. I fired at the lead swan and down he came. I had that swan mounted and he is now standing at the entrance to our beach house on Bald Head Island.

One year I was hunting in Gilbert Brickhouse's blind and, about 1,000 yards to my left, Bill Miller was hunting. I saw a flock of swan go by his blind; I heard one shot, but two fell. The next year in the same blind Bill Miller Jr., shot one time and got two swan. This was very unusual; especially father and son two years in a row.

One day I was hunting with Charlie Boyles. We were in a blind with our backs to a 25 mile per hour wind. A duck came over from our back, flying with the wind very high. Charlie said, "He's too high." I said, "I think I can get him with my Winchester." I raised up and fired and the duck folded up and fell. The wind was blowing so hard the duck fell about 100 yards out. The guide went over and picked the duck up out of the water. Charlie said, "What kind of shells are you using?" He couldn't believe I was using two and a half inch low power shells. I never use high power shells.

One day I was hunting with Ed Grimsley. We were on a point blind. A flock of about eight green wing teal were flying over. The guide said, "They're way too high and the wind's blowing way too hard for you to hit them." I took my old faithful shotgun and fired one shot; down came three ducks. It's strange how sometimes it's hard to miss and other times you can't hit the best of shots. One day three ducks came straight into the blind. We each shot three times and didn't hit one duck. The guide laughed at us. We told him to use his gun and shoot the next bunch. When the next bunch came over we threw up our guns as if to shoot, but didn't. The guide shot three times and didn't get a feather. We had our laugh.

Judd Sherman was a very good shot for a Yankee. When you hunted with him you had to shoot fast and, when the duck fell, say, "I got him." They say I have the fastest "I got him" of all the hunters.

On one hunt, Paul Snipes brought with him a 410 shot gun which was sawed off to make a pistol. He and Dr. Sy Gray were hunting together. A duck landed in the decoys and Sy asked Paul if he could use the 410 pistol to shoot the duck. Paul says, "Sure" and hands him the pistol. Sy put it up to his face like you would hold a shot gun to your shoulder. We don't know whether he hit the duck or not. When he shot the gun, it kicked, blacked his eye, and bloodied his nose. We all laughed, but it was not funny.

I hunted with Dr. Sam Hart several times. Sam was a very good shot. When he shot a duck he usually hit it. Dr. Bill Donald was hunting with Brickhouse one year. We all came in from hunting, showered and were ready to eat dinner and Bill hadn't come in. Colon went out looking for him. We were worried. This went on until late at night. They finally found Brickhouse and Bill blown down the sound toward the bridge at Point Harbor. This is where Currituck Sound meets Albemarle Sound. Brickhouse had run aground with his motor and got sand in it so it wouldn't run. The wind was blowing very hard to the south. They were firing a shot about every fifteen minutes. It was so dark this was the only way they could be located. After this episode Bill just wanted to hunt the pond behind the lodge. [You have to remember in those days we had no radios or cell phones. You were on your own. If you didn't come in, somebody would come look for you because we all knew where everybody was hunting. If you didn't have a light, shooting the gun and the fire coming out of the barrel was about the only way anybody could find you if you were out of your blind. Personally, I always had a flashlight, a box of matches in a jar to keep them dry and a flare or two. I kept all this in a plastic fishing box to keep them dry. And an anchor. I also had a 4hp motor on my skiff in addition to the 20hp. I still have that 4hp as a backup on my skiff.—TM]

One day Bill Miller and Judd Sherman were hunting with John Dennis as their guide. Bill liked to take a nap when there were no ducks flying, so he was asleep. Judd took Bill's gun and put a flare shell in it. A duck came in and landed in the decoys. Bill jumped up, picked up his gun, and fired at the duck. Fire flew out of his gun almost to the duck. Bill jumped back and said, "What the hell?!?" Judd and John were laughing so hard they could hardly stand up.

Worth Bowman was my C.P.A. when I started Purcell Supply Co. He was one of the best. You could ask him any question about taxes or tax laws and he would answer you on the spot. He didn't say, "I'll look it up and give you an answer tomorrow." Worth had back trouble and would hunt the pond behind the lodge. He would lay on his back on this wide plank and look for ducks. Worth had a brother who worked for me as a pipe fitter. He was one of the smartest persons that ever worked for me. He could work out about any math problem in his head. He'd been in the merchant marines. He'd traveled over the world and had a small farm in Randolph County. He was a very interesting person to talk with. He said he lived like the rich folks, only in reverse. He had heat in the summer and cooling in the winter. One morning he didn't show up for work. I called Worth and asked him to go check on him; he'd always been a very responsible worker. Worth found that he'd been shot and was dead. The Randolph County Sheriff said that he had shot himself. In talking with Worth about his brother, I don't believe it was suicide. Worth got the S.B.I. to check on the angle and distance the shot was fired. They stated that it was impossible for him to have shot himself. The Randolph County coroner liked to call a murder or accident suicide, so they could close the case.

The first year Bill Pruitt was invited to come on our duck hunt, he had fried oysters for dinner along with several drinks, to the point that he was sick and up most of the night. This was one thing we didn't put up with. Ed Grimsley and I had a big discussion before we invited him again. Bill became one of our better hunters. Bill flew his twin engine plane, which could hold six passengers. I'd fly with him. We would leave the Piedmont airport and fly east to Whiteville. We'd land at a small airport, and pick up Dick Crutchfield, one of Bill's good customers. Then we would fly to Elizabeth City. Before landing, we would buzz the lodge so Dorothy Grandy would know to come pick us up.

One time it was a beautiful day, after we picked up Dick we flew over Myrtle Beach. Then we followed the coastline all the way north. We flew over Bald Head Island. I could see my house. We flew over Carolina Beach, Wrightsville Beach, Cape Look Out, Cape Hatteras, and Currituck Sound. We flew so low over the sound we could see the ducks and geese getting up off the water. We were flying over 200 miles an hour. It was a beautiful sight to see.

One year Jim Slone and I hunted together. Altis Outlaw was our guide. The first day we hunted with him he split us up. He put me in a blind on one point and Jim on another point. I had a few ducks fly by and a few good shots. Jim had several shots. All of a sudden there were 50 to 100 ducks all around me. The guide said, "Let them fly around and some of

Hunting and Fishing Lodge on Mainland Currituck

them will come back around for a better shot." They flew over to where Jim was sitting. There were ducks all around him. Jim started shooting the whole bunch. He was so excited with so many ducks he didn't hit one duck. The next day we hunted a different blind with the same guide. There was very little shooting until late afternoon. The guide split us up and sent me out to a patch of brush about 150 feet from the blind. All of a sudden the sky was full of mallard ducks. We got our limit in about 30 minutes.

After the hunt we went back to the lodge. Everybody had a shave and a shower. The bull was so deep you had to pull up your pants legs. We all had a drink or two, then it was time for oysters. We went outside to a building behind the lodge where there was a long table made out of two sheets of 4x8 plywood. The oysters were hot from a steam maker. Colon would take a bushel of hot steamed oysters and dump them out in the middle of the table. There was plenty of melted butter, hot sauce and ketchup. We had a glove and oyster knife. We ate until we had enough. Then we went in the lodge and washed up for dinner. We all stood around the table until everyone was there. We had the blessing, which we always did before each meal, and then sat down to dinner. It was family style. When we finished, we needed to take a walk. It didn't matter how cold it was or what kind of weather we had.

When we came in from the hunt we always put our ducks, geese and swan on the back porch to be cleaned. I always liked to see what kind and how many ducks were killed. One day a hunter came in with a marsh rabbit. Another time one brought in a nutria.

The dinner Saturday night was always a meal to remember. There were silver candelabra with candles burning. All other lights were turned off after the meal. In came Dorothy and Colon with flaming jubilees. One day Paul Snipes brought 150 proof moonshine back from the mountains. He soaked some cherries in this moonshine, and I had them in a bowl. I was sitting just to the left of Ed Grimsley. He loved the cherries jubilee. When he turned his head I'd put a couple of these in his bowl. We kept talking and I kept putting the cherries in his bowl until all the cherries were gone. He said, "Hey, this jubilee is great!" To this day he never knew we were spiking his jubilee.

My first hunt on Currituck Sound was by an invite from Ed Grimsley. He loved this hunt, Caroland Farms, and Currituck Sound. He was a great sportsman and gentleman.

Years later Ed was sick and the doctor said it was just a matter of time before the end. I went to see Ed's wife and asked if Ed was up to it. I was told that Ed was in a coma and had been that way all day. Mrs. Grimsley asked if I'd like to see him and I said, "Yes." We went into his bedroom; she got close to Ed's ear and said, "Ed, Purcell is here." Ed opened his eyes and said, "Purcell, I sure am glad to see you." I said, "Ed, I just wanted to see you and say hello. I don't want to bother you." Ed said, "You won't bother me, I want to talk with you." We talked about hunting and our hunting group. Ed said that our hunting trips were the most enjoyable times of his life. He thanked me and said, "Purcell, it won't be long now." Ed went back in a coma and died a few hours later. Our hunts went on, but nobody ever sat at the head of the table after he was gone.

Colon and Dorothy Grandy employed a lot of men to guide either hunting or fishing or both in Currituck County. The following is a list that Dorothy gave me of the men who guided there at Caroland Farm at one time or another. If anybody was left out, it was not intentional.

Colon Grandy Sr.	Sid Wright Sr.
Colon Grandy Jr.	Sid Wright Jr.
Billy Grandy	Watson Stuart
Elmer Merrell	Billie Rose
Bud Lupton	Wade Sanderlin
Meture Lupton	Jack Guard
Bootie Spruill	Frankie Helms
John Dennis	Mike Mercer
Blanton Saunders	Alfred Everett
Wilton Outlaw	William Wright
Clarence Beasley	Thurman Sears
Rupert Parker	Graff Beasley
Gilbert Brickhouse	Bucky (Larry) Williams
Cecil Brickhouse	Warren Austin
Altis Outlaw	Ray Matusko
Sammy Walker	Bill Minton
Frank Carter	Eddie Walston
Tony Ballance	Dailey Williams
Cuffee (Norman) Lindsey	Nathan Cartwright

Bootie Spruill on Guiding Fishing Parties

I asked Bootie to tell me a little about his guiding experience at Caroland Farm. Bootie was first guiding for his mother-in-law, Bertha Gregory, before she started nursing and stopped taking in hunters and fishermen. Then he started guiding for Caroland Farm.

He told Colon there were two people who, if they ever asked for him, he was not going to take them: Dr. Fortney and Dr. Gray. The reason was they would book for three days, and nine times out of ten they would fish one day and leave, and that would make him vacant for two days.

I asked Bootie what was the most bass he ever caught in one day when all that grass was here. He said they caught over two hundred one day. He said his thumb got right raw from putting it in the bass' mouth to take the hook out.

One time Bootie had a Dr. Fortesque from Kernersville, and his nephew, Frank, that liked to fly fish. For some reason the bass around the shoreline quit biting with fly bait. You could just catch them with a feather bait, underwater bait, so Bootie told him if he wanted to be sure to catch some fish to bring about five dozen minnows with him. He went down to Colon's and got the minnows. Bootie had some reed poles right there in the boat.

He went up there around the Gull Rock, and there was about an acre (about like a pond) right in that grass that was clear of grass. He went in there and poled them around the edge of it. They were fishing devil-horses, and every once in a while they'd catch one. Bootie said, "Let's go over here in one of these little holes and try 'em." He said he got over there by a little hole and stobbed her down (tied the boat out). They put minnows on the cane poles, and he told them to drop them right down in that hole. Bootie said, "Now you'll get right." He got him another cane pole and started hitting that water with the tip end of the pole. It wasn't long before that cork went out of sight. The doctor said, "You sure busted my bubble when you started beating that water. I thought you were going to scare every fish out of Currituck Sound." He said they sat right there and caught eight or ten out of that one hole.

There was a guy who stayed at Caroland Farm from Knoxville, Tennessee, named Bill Laddermill that was head of a group that came down here fishing. Bootie said sometimes he'd bring as many as eighteen people. He said it got to the point that when he'd come down and say, "Let's go to (such and such a place) tomorrow," and Bootie would say, "Alright." He said he'd go try it, and if there wasn't anything there he'd move him somewhere else.

Bootie Spruill, guide, standing on the end of his pier with his hands on his hips. The others are sportsmen. *Dorothy Grandy.*

He was a good fisherman, but he had one of these Johnson Reels and that thing was big around and heavy. If he got a big fish on it, he'd have to crank the handle back for the drag to work. By the time he did that, the bass had either broke his line or something.

One time he came down and said, "I got a reel here ain't no bass in Currituck Sound gonna' break." Bootie said this man liked to fish with a jitterbug. He was right down south of Murray Elliot's, coming up that shoreline and by and by that water exploded. He was cutting the water with the line and broke the line. Bootie said, "Bill, I thought you said you had one that wouldn't break that line." He was hot. He threw that rod and reel down in the bottom of the boat. Bootie said it was seventeen-pound line, and when that fish popped it, it sounded like a twenty-two rifle going off. Bootie said he'd seen him lose some big fish, and he kept telling him, "Bill, if you'll get you an Ambassador reel they've got good drags on 'em, and you just won't lose 'em with that." The reason he didn't get it was he didn't think he could throw it without getting backlashes, but you can tighten 'em down so they won't backlash. He caught a many a bass. I always left from my house to guide and I carried him one time. The fishing had slacked up across the sound, so I said, "Bill, I'm gonna' carry you to a new place. It'll take us a while to get there." I went up to Cedar Island Bay. You could catch fish up there, but you didn't know what was going to be on the hook when you brought it in. It might be a pike, it might be a grenal or it might be a bass.

Hunting and Fishing Lodge on Mainland Currituck

They always had a pot down there at the lodge as to who caught the most fish and most of the time he'd win the pot.

Bootie said that one time Bill brought a fellow with him named Larry, who had black lung disease from working in a coal mine. Bootie said, "Larry, are you gonna' cast or minnow fish?" He said, "Give me that cane pole." He started out with a cane pole, and Bootie didn't move but twice. Bill was fishing with a devil-horse or jitterbug (a lot of time you'd catch rock on a devil-horse). Bootie said he caught a rock on a devil-horse up there one time that weighed ten pounds.

Bootie said they fished that five dozen minnows up in about two hours. They said, "Let's go back in and get some more minnows." We were right there in front of the house, so it didn't take long to do it. We slipped in there and came right back out. I think it was fifty-six we caught that day.

There was a streak that went right up the middle of the sound about fifty feet wide that there weren't no grass in. I don't know why, but there was fish in it, I can tell you that.

Then Bootie and I were talking about the milfoil. It went like it came; all of a sudden it was gone. We think maybe the salt water had something to do with it.

Bootie said he caught a bass with a mouth full of leeches. He carried him over to Elizabeth City to Marine Fisheries, and they said they were saltwater leeches. You'd think a fish couldn't eat with his mouth full of leeches, but he said he'd seen them when there would be scars in their mouth and wouldn't be a leech in there.

Bootie said he saw that the bass were dropping off, and he and John Dennis decided to quit guiding bass fishermen. They started getting them some crab pots. They decided they could make more money crabbing in two hours than they could make all day shoving that pole.

Dorothy and Colon Grandy had many prominent guests stay at the lodge. I'm not going to begin to name them. When Dorothy writes her memoirs, I'm sure she will tell you all about them.

I wrote this book to preserve the history of the wooden boats, mainly inboard motorboats that were built and used in Currituck. Because of fiberglass boats and high-horsepower outboard motors, they are now a thing of the past.

I also wanted to preserve the history of commercial fishing off the beach and haul seining in Currituck Sound, as well as guides poling sport fishermen around the sound for largemouth bass. They are all things that are gone forever.

Travis Morris

About the Author

Travis Morris was born in Coinjock, North Carolina, in 1932 (in the same house his mother was born in on April 3, 1908). He was the only child of Chester and Edna Boswood Morris. His father was an attorney and later a Superior Court judge. While practicing law, Judge Morris represented many of the old hunt clubs in Currituck County, which is how Travis came by much of his firsthand knowledge. These hunt clubs owned nearly all of Currituck Beach from the late 1800s up until the beginning of development in 1968. Travis served three years in the U.S. Coast Guard and then spent a year and a half at Campbell College. Early on, he farmed and had a long-distance trucking company; he also guided sportsmen and managed Monkey Island Hunting Lodge. In 1983, he cofounded Piney Island Club with John High, which is still in existence and of which he is still a member. For the past forty-three years, he has been in the real estate business.

Travis served on the Currituck County Planning Board for eight years and has been a member of the Currituck County Historical Society for as many years as he can remember. Even though he has been writing recollections for pleasure for many years, he never dreamed he would have nine books published. He has thoroughly enjoyed sharing his memories with the public.